Mother Teacher

From the memoirs of Lois Callaway
Missionary to the Mien People of S.E. Asia

D1124814

Joyce Bhang

Mother Teacher

From the memoirs of Lois Callaway
Missionary to the Mien People of S.E. Asia

by
Joyce Bhang

Lois with Mien children at entrance to Chiangkham Refugee Center 1979

Lois Callaway – 1990's

In Appreciation

C.W. & Lois Callaway have expressed their
deep gratitude to God for His constant care and
to their many co-workers and supporters including:

Fellow missionaries- Dorothy Uhlig,
Imogene Williams, Mel & June Byers

Forwarding Agents- Alice Callaway (C.W.'s mother),
Genevieve Webb, and Benette Rhoades

And 30 + Christian Churches/Churches of Christ providing funds,
encouragement, and prayer.

To my Mien friends and to my family.
Thank you for your patience.

—Joyce Bhang

By way of introduction ...

Most every American has heard of the Vietnam War. What many Americans do not know is that this war had messily spilled over into the neighboring countries of Vietnam. Quiet mountain villages of Laos were bombed. Young Laotian boys barely taller than the firearms they carried were enlisted by the C.I.A. to fight the communists. This was the Silent War; the war in Laos that by official U.S. declaration, did not exist. Refugees fleeing the communists were crammed into filthy barbed-wire camps in Thailand.

The camps were bursting with the sick, the hungry, the dying, and the hopeless. **Lois Callaway** was an American missionary in Thailand at that time. **Yoon Choy Saechao** was a young village boy in Laos whose life was forever changed by the Silent War. It was in the stench of the camp that their lives intersected, and Yoon Choy found salvation.

I was privileged to sit and listen to both their stories. History is best heard from those who were there. These two stories have become a singular story of crossing cultures and survival. It is as much a tribute to Lois Callaway as to the Mien people like Yoon Choy, whom she loved and served. One person with a heart inclined toward the will of God, can effect change. Lois Callaway showed me that this can be true.

LOIS NADINE ELKERTON arrived in this world in a simple sod home in Adena, Morgan County, Colorado on November 24, 1921. She distinguished herself in Fort Morgan (CO) High School and in that city in journalism and anticipated a career in that field.

She was active in her church youth group and there felt the call of the Lord on her life for foreign mission service. She thus entered Phillips University in Enid, Oklahoma. There she met C.W. Callaway. After a 2-year courtship they married in Enid on May 28. 1942. They ministered in Glencoe, Oklahoma. While continuing studies at Cincinnati (Ohio) Bible Seminary they ministered to Syria and Bethel Christian Churches near Orleans, Indiana.

They first went abroad in Dec. 1946 for a year's study in missionary medicine and Burmese in London, England. After a frustrating 6 months of trying in vain to extend their visas in Burma they served a year in Kunming, Yunnan, W. China. Forced from China by the communist takeover they went on to Thailand where they arrived on Oct. 18, 1949. Most events in this book occurred in Thailand. Throughout their ministry they have been supported by several local congregations of Christian Churches and Churches of Christ.

C.W. & Lois have 2 sons born in America, one daughter born in China, and a son and daughter born in Thailand. Lois died in an automobile accident near Napa, CA on Sept. 5, 1996.

Joyce Bhang

*Lois on her grandfather's
scales (1923)*

*Lois' high school portrait
(1938)*

Table of Contents

Chapter 1

The Five-Colored Dog

About 900 B.C. during the Western Zhou Dynasty in China, there lived a good king named Bien Hung. He was ruler over a peaceful people, rich in a culture lavish with silver and intricate brocade. The people were called the Mien.

Neighboring kings, eyeing the idyllic settlement of the Mien were driven by jealousy and greed into the madness of conquest. Emperor Gao Hsin was one such enemy. He schemed daily to possess for himself the riches of the Mien.

Although a swift river stood between them, Bien Hung knew it was not long before they would fall prey to their enemy. He petitioned the heavens for help. In his prayer, he asked for a hero for the people. He pledged half of his kingdom and his third daughter in marriage.

"Send us a hero," the king implored, "A hero who has the bravery, strength, and cunning to kill Gao Hsin and bring me his head."

Bien Hung's prayer was answered but not in the way he had anticipated. His own guard dog, Li Daa Hu, came to him one day, saying he would be the one to kill Emperor Gao Hsin. Bien Hung looked at the strong jaws, muscular legs, and unusual five-colored coat of his dog. His initial shock gave way to confidence and he smiled. He honored his dog's faithfulness.

"Go and save the Mien people."

Li Daa Hu left his master's side, looked across the river to the palace of his enemy and jumped in. The currents were swift and the river rolled and lashed about like a demon's tongue, but Li Daa Hu crossed the great river. Slowly pulling himself from the water, now wet and shivering, Li Daa Hu used the last of his strength to climb up to the palace where sympathetic servants let him in and fed him. The food was rich and tasty, and the palace was warm and comfortable. Li Daa Hu was given a thick blanket on which to rest. One day, the emperor saw the mottled dog and called him over. Li Daa Hu went obediently to the emperor, turned quickly, and sat like a sentry at his feet, barely brushing the hem of his brocade robe. The emperor's eyes widened, impressed by this show of loyalty. But had the emperor looked into the eyes of the dog, he would have seen the flames of death. Li Daa Hu had not forgotten why he was now in the palace.

"This dog will be my companion in battle," he smiled. There were others who were not as sure, and eyed the dog with side-ways glances.

For three months, the five-colored dog worked to gain the trust of the emperor. He growled and showed his sharp teeth to anyone who came too close to the emperor, or approached too quickly. He walked with him by day, sat at his feet, quietly listening to the evil plottings against his master, and slept by the foot of his bed.

"Be sure that the emperor is never alone with the five-colored dog," the commanding officer told his guards.

One day a palace official ventured a direct accusation. "That is your enemy's dog. I recognize the five-colored coat!"

Emperor Gao Hsin only laughed and said, "My foolish enemy Bien Hung must be easily defeated now. Even his dog has left his side."

The emperor eventually dismissed his personal guards, confident of the dog's protection and loyalty. Late one night, Li Daa Hu found himself alone with the emperor. He leaped onto his bed and with his powerful jaws, tore Gao Hsin's head off.

When Li Daa Hu once again braved the strong river currents, this time with the enemy's head in his teeth, he arrived home triumphant. The threat of war was over.

Li Daa Hu was a hero. King Bien Hung remembered his promise to give the Mien hero his daughter in marriage, but feared the shame that would follow his daughter for being wed to a dog. His daughter assured him that all would be well and so he gave his blessing and provided a place for them to live, high in the remote mountains. The heavens honored the king for keeping his word. Li Daa Hu was an angel dog. Once on the mountain, standing amidst a wrap of wispy white clouds, Li Daa Hu was transformed into a man. Li Daa Hu became father to six sons and six daughters. All of whom eventually married and became the progenitors of the twelve clans of the Mien people, who have lived for many centuries in the high mountains of Asia. They are known today by these names:

Bienh = Phan/Saephan/Saepharn
Leiz = Lee/Saelee
Zeuz = Chao/Saechao
Dangc = Saetern/Saeteurn
Zanh = Zin/Saechin
Lorh = Saelaw/Saelor/Saelo
Yangh = Saeyang
Zaengc = Ziou/Zuo/Saechou/Saechuo
Waang = Hu/Saewang
Dorngh = Tong/Saetong/Saeto
Liouh = Luei/Saeleo/Saeliew
Bungz = Borng/Fongc/Saefong

There was no hero to be found for the Mien after the angel dog, Li Daa Hu. Historically, the tribes were scattered throughout Asia, escaping successive encroachments and banishments by neighboring kingdoms. With each uprooting, the tribes eventually found themselves scattered throughout the world. Somehow, they maintained their culture and the strong tribal ties. They are Mien, which translated, means "the people."

It is said that a thousand years ago, there was a terrible drought. The skies closed up for six years. The hardened earth, parched and barren, cracked in huge gaping rifts, big enough to swallow up a cow. The Mien elderly withered into the arid soil, and the young had no strength to stand. The weakened cries of mourning and pain would die out only to usher in more of the same. Convinced that the rains would not return, the Mien left their homes and crowded onto ten ships in search of a kinder sky. They set their course by the clouds. Even the slightest white whisper in the sky gave them hope.

The king gave his people the responsibility of guarding the only the books written in the Mien language. As they sailed, they faced horrible storms called nzi-aaux-jieqv or black storms. The boats were pounded by the enormous waves. They feared for their lives. They feared for their precious books. Rather than have the sea swallow the books, they ate the books themselves. The Mien written language was gone.

As the Mien kept their eyes on the skies, the shifting clouds led them farther and farther apart. In time, the clouds scattered the Mien to Laos, Vietnam, and Thailand, and to distant parts of China. But still they would remember their culture and heritage, even without books, without their written language. The Mien stubbornly maintained their history with a strong oral tradition and remained "the people." [1]

Set apart as a special tribe several hundred years ago, the Chinese government recognized the unique presence of the Mien, and granted them exclusive privileges and rights to land ownership. The government established the Mien Charter, an official document which declared the uncontestable freedom of the Mien Tribe.

Many Mien settled in the mountains of Laos. This was Yoon Choy's home. Yoon Choy grew up in a quiet mountain village, a clustering of boarded shacks with thatched roofs, nestled amidst the highest trees, a two-day walk from the base of the mountain. As a ten-year old boy, he helped with the rice fields which were cultivated down in the lowlands. He cared for the water buffalo, horses, pigs and chickens daily. He watched over his younger siblings. A large, teeming fishpond provided water for his long-horned buffalo.

When the rice harvest was good, the family worked for days in the lowland field, staying off the mountain for days at a time, sleeping in a nearby shelter, cooking rice for their meals in an extra iron pot, which was always left in the lowlands by the field. The earth provided their needs, and since the spirits were happy, there was no serious illness.

Their idyllic existence teetered like a crystalline dream on the edge of a war-infested world. During the Vietnam War, Yoon Choy's lush green country of Laos was viewed as one giant, strategically placed air strip; a means to an end, eventually to be consumed, expended, depleted.

"There is no war in Laos," was the official statement broadcast to the general public in the United States, yet the United States government secretly battled against the Pathet Lao and North Vietnamese forces. The Silent War. For the C.I.A.'s covert operations, specialized forces like the Ravens, and the visceral intuition and passion of the Air America pilots were employed. But when the United States needed more manpower, they turned to the locals; the fiercely courageous Hmong tribe and other tribes like the Mien. The communist insurgents quickly realized that to take away their enemy's manpower was as simple as decimating their villages.

When Yoon Choy was ten, his father gave him a gun to carry even as he tended the chickens. Yoon Choy's peaceful world was close to shattering. He started to feel the unease in his chest, but still he tended his animals, and rode his buffalo, and watched his younger brothers.

Destruction came one day in the midst of a plentiful rice harvest. After spending several days in the lowlands harvesting their rice, Yoon Choy spotted a group of soldiers from the Lao Communist Army. A smooth-faced soldier with his head thrown back in an arrogant stare warned them that they would be next. He took a large basket of freshly harvested rice, and made Yoon Choy's father carry it to their jeep. Yoon Choy saw airplanes circling about, their throbbing engines sending an ominous signal echoing through the quiet green. For some days they had seen smoke rising from the neighboring hillsides. No one had need of a fire so large that the smoke would loom up beyond the treetops. The smoke was from entire villages engulfed in flames.

Yoon Choy's family continued with their harvest, looking up occasionally. When they were finally ready to make their way back up the mountain, they were stopped along the road by the sight of their neighbor, running wildly towards them down the steep trail.

"You must not go back to the village. The communists are

coming. The entire village is moving up to the next mountain."

They turned immediately and ran, leaving their home behind.

"I want to get my buffalo," said Yoon Choy, "Who will take care of my buffalo?" His voice was swallowed up in a chorus of panicked voices and the dull thumping of running feet. Yoon Choy was sent back to the rice field to retrieve their rice pot. Two hundred villagers were displaced that day, scattered throughout the mountains. Quickly, straight into the thickest parts of the mountain jungles they pushed their way through the brush. When they stopped, they were in the safety of trees that were so tall that the smoke curling up from their campfire got lost in the canopy of tangled branches. Yoon Choy helped his father and brothers make tents out of banana leaves. He thought of his animals, the buffalo, his horses, pigs, and chickens running about with no one to feed them, and wanted to go home.

Each time he had to reprimand his younger brothers to be quiet, each time he had to search the forest for things to eat, or felt the tightness in his chest when the noises and shadows of the jungle took on human shape, the reality shook him - he would never return home. He missed his animals and he cried for them at night under the banana leaf tent. The family stayed hidden in the mountains for six months until they feared discovery again and fled to a nearby Hmong village that was under American protection. Armed soldiers walked back and forth.

At twelve years Yoon Choy saw his first white men and learned how to shoot their big guns. At fifteen he was paid and trained by the American government to shoot the communists. Yoon Choy fought in the so-called Silent War. It wasn't silent for him. At twenty-five, the unknown country he served became his new home; by then Yoon Choy was saved. And when he speaks of his salvation, he speaks of Mother Teacher.

Chapter 2

Kay Sah Muh She Boo

1960. In the midst of the scare of communism, atomic wars, and mistrust, there stood a bright, opinionated, apron-clad woman named Lois Callaway. She lived boldly in Asia when others cowered in their yellow formica kitchens as their husbands dug bomb shelters in their backyards. Though there were some scary hard times, she would say that her life was full and good as God is good. She would say that she was an ordinary woman. She would say that her story was really quite the same as yours; laughing and weeping, running and plodding, long-suffering and sometimes as high-flying as the wispy mountain clouds of Thailand. She would say that she probably got angry more often than you think that a missionary would or should. But she did.

When God talked to Lois, even as a child, she was inclined to listen. When she was just a youth, He told her to come on up to the front of the church and receive His everlasting love and forgiveness, and that's what she did. When she was in college, He told her to find a tribe that had never heard about Him before, that's what Lois did. He didn't tell her that He was going to give her a tour of Asia on the way, but that's what He did.

And then there was this matter of marriage. For three years at every mission meeting since she started Phillips University in 1939, she sat across the table from a tall, sweet Texan with serious eyes so intense they could poke a hole right through you. His passion to serve the Lord was as great as all of Texas. Lois knew they shared a strong and undeniable heart-call to serve overseas. His name was Charley Watley Callaway Jr. In Texas they called him "C.W." Lois called him "Dub."

She heard God calling them together just a mite quicker than he did. C.W. was fond of saying, "She chased me for two years until I caught her."

"Don't you think it's about time we got married, Dub?" As determined as he was, he still needed a little prodding in some areas.

"That sounds like a good idea," he said. So they married on May 28, 1942.

Soon after, Dub and Lois singled out the Rawang Tribe in Burma to be their mission field. They printed a small pamphlet, Introductory Bulletin of Northern Burma Christian Mission. The perilous nature of their mission was highlighted by these words: "...in the light of the fact that Burma offers one of the most deadly climates in which American missionaries can undertake to work, medical experts will be duly asked to pass upon the physical fitness of Mr. and Mrs. Callaway to attempt the extremely difficult task they are planning."

Often however, the more "deadly climate" was found in the subtleties of discouragement from the churchiest of sources. Lois faced glancing comments about their ignorance of the political world climate. There were whisperings about those Callaways: Did they know? Communists are trying to take over the world. Would God truly call His children to a place of danger?

Joe McCarthy had taught the citizens of the United States well. Suspiciously eyeing the world through pink-colored lenses, Americans were convinced that communist spies had infiltrated higher government, and every true-blue American was in danger. McCarthy's alcohol-laced voice was a contagious barrage of hysterical rhetoric. Americans were taking cover. The air raid sirens at noon became a familiar rehearsal for the communist terror that never came. Why in heaven's name, Lois, would you want to go to Burma of all places where the communists probably will be waiting for you with guns?

While most Americans admittedly trembled under the gaze of communism's red face, Lois Callaway stared back. Unblinking. She knew God's call. Communism or no, the Callaways had a very simple confidence in the Lord's commission. It even said so in writing: "Mr. and Mrs. Callaway are grounded in the simple faith of the Gospel of our Lord." There it was in their letter of recommendation: Simple faith. The decision to go overseas was simply made.

Lois was direct and said what was on her mind, and on her mind was the Lord's voice telling her to go. There would be no deterring the tall, lanky Texan either. So, forging against the tide of fear, the Callaways gave all they had of their time, their money, and all of their efforts to study abroad to ready themselves for missionary life.

In 1948 Lois held the hands of her two young sons, Lelan and Mark and stepped foot on the hard Burmese soil. She had spent fourteen months in England to learn the Burmese language. Here now was her final exam.

CW and Lois with Lelan and Mark in London (1948)

In England, her Burmese language professor was a former British Official in Burma while it was still a British colony. He had a fine reputation of having mastered Burmese. The professor insisted on giving periodic oral tests himself, even though her tutor was a native speaker. During one such exam, he was highly indignant when he found that she had not learned an essential Burmese phrase.

"I find it difficult to believe that you have not yet learned, "*Kay sah muh she boo.*"

"What does it mean?" This must be a critical survival phrase.

He answered Lois in a very deliberate, carefully articulated English tone, "It means very simply, 'It doesn't matter.'"

The disbelief puffed out in her face and widened her eyes as he continued to insist that the phrase was the most important thing to learn in any Asian language. It doesn't matter? Lois needed to survive in a foreign country on one semester of language learning, and the most important phrase to take with her was, "It doesn't matter?" Well, it did matter to Lois, everything mattered; her time, her energy, her family... but she learned the phrase nonetheless.

As Lois settled into her new life and home in Burma, she and C.W.found themselves quickly caught up in the challenge of acquiring permanent visas. The Kachin Minister was welcoming to the Callaways. The new independent Central Burmese government, however, was not. Despite special petitions by the Kachin Minister, their residence visas were summarily refused. The Burmese door slammed shut after only four months. The Callaways were forced to change their best-laid plans and leave quickly under pressure from the government. Her professor would have wanted her to reply, "*Kay sah muh she boo,*" but it did matter to her. At that moment the glibness of that phrase infuriated her, but before she could speak, as if on cue, C.W. responded with a soft word.

"We've just come across an entire ocean to serve tribal people," said C.W. "We'll just have to find another tribe. We'll move to China. There are tribes similar to the Rawang living along the Burma-China border."

Lois smiled. Her husband had found an inroad to the true meaning of "*Kay sah muh she boo.*" "It doesn't matter, just move on." It was agreed, but Lois was totally unprepared for this new culture. She was frustrated. They had studied Burmese for months, but didn't know a word of Chinese. The thought of the wasted months of Burmese language training they had spent in England were quickly pushed aside, and they proceeded with their travel plans. The Callaways knew that the Morses, another Christian Church missionary family, lived in Kunming, China. They hurriedly made plans to contact them and move to the country next door.

"I'll stay back and bring our supplies by train to Mandalay, then head over to Kunming," said C.W.

"The boys and I will be expecting you within two weeks. I'll be waiting. I love you, Dub."

Lois took her two young sons, Lelan and Mark, and flew out of Burma in August. As the plane took off, the first shots of battle were fired in a heated and extended conflagration between the Burmese government and the communists.

Lois arrived safely in Kunming. She anxiously waited for C.W. to arrive as the days slowly churned into weeks. Lois occupied her worried mind by starting the practical language acquisition method of "market and kitchen" language study. "*Sahn shir wahn*," were the first words she learned. The words meant "30,000," which was the exchange rate for the American dollar at that time.

Back in Burma, with so much to organize and pack on his own, C.W. missed the train. As he packed up the luggage, he listened with weary resignation as the train pulled away from the station. Letting out a frustrated sigh, he wondered when the next train would be leaving for Mandalay. The next day, he checked the schedule and found that there were no more scheduled trips on that route. The train that headed out from the station to Mandalay the day before, the train that C.W. would have been on, never arrived. A bridge had been bombed and the train crashed, killing many passengers that day. Because news traveled slowly, Lois did not hear of the train incident until well after she received a letter from C.W. telling her of his change in plans.

C.W. was held up in Rangoon for over three weeks. Finally, he was able to hitch up with a convoy of trucks with a military escort to Pegu and continued by train to Mandalay. Armed only with a small book of useful Chinese phrases that he had purchased in Rangoon, C.W. boarded a truck at the Chinese border.

"Where are we?"

"What is that?"

"Is that edible?"

"Where is the bathroom?"

Six weeks after they had parted, C.W. arrived in Kunming from Rangoon, weary, but fluent in basic Chinese. He also became very adept at his own version of international sign language.

***Christian Church missionaries in
Kunming, China – March 1949***
*Back Row: L-R, <u>Mel Byers</u>, Ellis Back, <u>J. Russell Morse</u>,
<u>CW. Callaway</u>, <u>Robert Morse</u>, <u>Eugene Morse</u>, Bill Rees
3rd Row: Harold Taylor, Lora Banks Harrison,
<u>Imogene Williams</u>, <u>Mrs. Robert Morse</u>,
Mrs. Harry Randolph, Harry Randolph
2nd Row: Leland Taylor, Ruth Margaret Morse,
Mrs. Harold Taylor, <u>Mrs. J. Russell Morse</u>,
<u>Lois Callaway</u>, <u>Mrs. Eugene Morse</u>, Melba Rees
1st Row: Glen Taylor, <u>Mark & Lelan Callaway</u>
(Those underlined later served in Thailand)*

Detoured from Burma, but encouraged to be still in Asia, Lois pushed on with her studies of the Chinese language. They employed help and found residence in a Kunming suburb. After several months, Lois began to feel comfortable running a household having mastered certain useful phrases in Chinese. Confidently she called out phrases of greeting, and developed a rapport with her household help. They called her "Madame Tall."

A kind young Chinese man who worked with Lois finally got the courage to tell her something of importance. With a bit of embarrassment he began, "Madame Tall, I must tell you. When the gate bell rings, and you call out, *'Nah i go?'* I believe you want to say 'Who is it?', is that correct?"

"Yes, I do want to say 'Who is it?' is anything wrong?"

"Madame Tall, you are really saying, 'Which dog is it?'."

Then he explained there should be a level tone on go even though it was a question. Lois wished he had told her sooner, but she knew that he was too polite to embarrass her until they were better acquainted.

Lois loved China and her new friends, but this was not to be the last stop in her missionary travels. The communists were coming, and soon she felt the door to this country closing too, and sadly resigned herself to saying good-bye.

Lois and CW in
Chinese costume with
Mark and Joyce (1949)

In 1949, Lois gave birth to her third child, Joyce, in a Kunming missions hospital. While in Kunming, the Callaways banded together with several other missionaries. One of the missionaries was a young woman, Miss Imogene Williams who was also committed to tribal work. She chose to join the Callaways on their new venture. Two months later, the baby bundled and the boys packed up, the Callaways and Imogene flew to Hong Kong. In Hong Kong, they learned of work to be done in Thailand and boarded a ship in search of yet another tribe.

At daybreak October 18, 1949 the little ship Hoi Wong sailed 30 miles up the Chao Phya River to Bangkok. Lois found herself on this small chugging boat to yet another culture, another language, and another adventure. She stood on the small wooden deck with C.W. and her two young sons. At the other end of the railing she looked to Imogene and smiled. Lois held baby Joyce bundled tightly in her arms. As the greenery of the shoreline passed by, and she felt the rhythms of her own breathing and the surging of the struggling engine, Lois wondered if her call would ever be realized, the dream of working with tribal villagers that they might hear the loving voice of God as she so clearly did. There were tribal people in the mountains of Thailand—the Lisu, the Mien, the Hmong, but there were rumors that the communists might infiltrate this country's borders too.

The spires and smoke of Bangkok eventually came into view; Lois put aside her unsure thoughts of the future to face the present. She took a deep breath and reached over to hug her boys with her free hand.

Time eventually proved the Burmese language professor right. Sometime later while in North Thailand, Lois learned the real meaning of *"Kay sah muh she boo"* and the philosophy behind it. By Thai standards the Callaways were considered wealthy, and in that culture they were expected to hire domestic help. Lois had her own cook. Imagine that. One day, the cook broke one of her favorite dishes. Lois was upset. Being overseas has a way of making things from home more precious. Still steaming, Lois asked her, "How did this happen?" thinking that she would warn her against that kind of carelessness ever again. The cook's reply was the Northern Thai equivalent of *"Kay sah muh she boo." "Bor ben yahng,"* she said. "It doesn't matter." But it did.

*CW and Lois studying Thai
with Kru Tat (1950)*

Lois wanted her to apologize. She didn't. So Lois did nothing and fumed for a while more. After some thought she realized that uncaring attitude wasn't consistent with the cook's cooperative and helpful nature. It's in the English translation that misunderstanding occurred. The cook wasn't saying that it didn't matter that the dish was broken. She was only saying, "It is not worth dwelling upon" just like C.W. had pressed on to a new country when Burma closed and didn't sit there moping. Lois calmed herself and reasoned: she was a great cook, she had a way with greens. It's a good way of thinking.

"Kay sah muh she boo," even when there was no Burmese ear to hear it, became like a mantra to Lois; a part of her Asian acculturation. It doesn't matter. It really doesn't matter. Go on, just keep going on. The broken dish, the denied visa, the communist activity, *"Kay sah muh she boo."*

Chapter 3

Chiangkham

While the Callaways got settled in Thailand, the general public of the United States received an announcement that the Russians were now in possession of an atomic bomb. That kept the red glow of communism going like a warning buzzer. The bomb cast ominous shadows over the freshly garnered peace from World War II. With communism threatening many of Thailand's neighboring countries, the Thai looked upon the Callaways with some suspicion as they had just come from China and spoke some of that "communist" language rather well.

"You speak Chinese."

"Yes, we learned Chinese while in Kunming," Lois answered.

"The Chinese are communists." The implication was seared into their words.

"We are not communists." Lois offered, but knew that in order to be accepted, there was urgency to quickly acquire the Central Thai dialect. If the missionaries' physical appearance alone wasn't enough to make them an instant oddity, once they opened their mouths, they were eyed with an unblinking distrust reserved for revolutionaries. The spotlight was already on the great white people, now it was up to them to determine whether it would be the spotlight on celebrity who brings good news, or the search light that finds and condemns the escaped convict.

In February of 1950, C.W., together with an interpreter, traveled north to Chiangkham, a gathering place for many mountain tribes, in Chiang Rai province. C.W. went to see if their work for the Lord might be started there. From Chiang Mai, he traveled first by train, then by truck and a day by oxcart, and arrived at 8 o'clock in the evening, two days later. It was festival time with throngs of Thai and Lu people about as well as many Mien tribespeople, easily recognized by the intricate embroidery designs, and feathery red boa worn by the women. Here was a great need. It seemed God's will for them to begin in Chiangkham, so upon his return to Bangkok, the Callaways and Imogene started packing their bags.

Callaway family preparing to travel by truck,
Thailand (1951)

In the early morning hours of May 11, 1950 they arrived in Chiangkham. The villagers looked up from smoky fires and squatting stools and stared at the bizarre parade before them: three large, white missionaries, two little white boys, a small white baby, and three oxcarts. Lois wanted to wave. "Falang" means "foreigner" in Thai. It also means "guava" which lends itself naturally to a few local jokes. News traveled quickly when "fresh" Falang arrived in the village.

The missionaries occupied a three-room shack in the middle of the village. Naturally curious about these great white visitors, the villagers, both young and old often peered in through the cracks in the walls at all times of the day. Lois' initial excitement over moving to Chiangkham was rapidly being replaced with the uneasiness of having her most private moments open for public viewing. A move into a two-story wooden house weeks later restored a modicum of her treasured privacy. She rapidly had to learn new rules, however, and to accept new values and new meanings to words like "respect" and "rudeness." Although she no longer had to check the cracks for prying eyes, she found herself constantly startled and sometimes angered by unexpected entrances by the neighbors. Then she learned that in Thailand, it was considered rude to begin to speak to someone before making eye contact first, much less banging on a door and yelling, so everyone entered unannounced, and sometimes quite abruptly.

There were times when a little warning beforehand would have been appreciated, but she survived. As she saw that her visitors were not embarrassed about their untimely entries, eventually neither was she, and later on, in deference to Lois, often the Thai cook would stand at the bedroom door and cough loudly in order to be recognized and give her warning.

Lois tried to use every opportunity to make friends with the adults and children alike, and found that food was an excellent point of commonality. The family consumed the local Thai favorites with enthusiasm. At 6 A.M. Lois would be up and about the open market, seeking out her favorite sweet rice vendor. Lois loved to watch her serve up the steamed sweet black or white rice. After a dollop of coconut cream, Lois chose from an assortment of toppings. The children loved dried fish with grated raw coconut. C.W. and Lois preferred coconut custard, grated raw coconut and poppy seeds. They acquired a taste for balls of sweet rice dipped in very hot sauce frequently seasoned with garlic and dried fish or fermented shrimp paste. Their Thai friends would grin widely as they watched their faces react to the spicy foods.

Over time, a number of other missionaries joined the Callaway family in Thailand in service to the Thai, Chinese, and several tribal groups. Dorothy Uhlig, a nurse from Oregon, and Imogene opened a Christian clinic in the Callaway's first home and the Callaways moved to another home nearby. This group became a close-knit family in ministry.

Nai Jan Ta, a Northern Thai, responded to the invitation to "taste Christ." After coming to faith in Christ, his enthusiasm overflowed. Persecution was a joy. He was a true overcomer. Lois was in awe at the purity of his faith and the commitment demonstrated in his life.

After walking eight miles from a Christian meeting one evening, Nai Jan Ta was met by his wife.

"While you have been away there has been a village meeting at the temple. The neighbors have been forbidden to have anything to do with us. They cannot even sell us rice if we are starving."

"Praise the Lord!" replied Nai Jan Ta, "Now we know we are the Lord's. There is a work of the Holy Spirit in this village and Satan opposes it."

This was true. People were understanding the freedom in Christ and were receiving His grace in neighboring villages. Nai Jan Ta persisted in his witness even when he knew angry jeers and threats awaited him. "I must tell them about the Lord God."

One day, Nai Jan Ta was shown an idol. It was an ancient family heirloom. The owner was very proud of it. It had eight hands. Two covered the eyes, two covered the ears, two the mouth, and two the abdomen.

Nai Jan Ta looked at it and asked, "Do you know the meaning of this idol?"

"Oh yes," replied the man. "It means 'hear no evil, see no evil, speak no evil, desire no evil."

"No," countered Nai Jan Ta, "This is a symbol of how the devil has blinded you to the Gospel. He has covered your ears so that you cannot hear, he has covered your eyes so you cannot see, your mouth so you cannot inquire, and your heart so you cannot receive the Lord Jesus. This idol has blinded your grandfather, and he passed it on to your father. It blinded him, and he passed it on to you. You will pass it on to your children and blind them. It is a very evil thing. You should throw it away and come to Christ before you are so blind you cannot." Nai Jan Ta stood firm in his urgency, but the man walked away.

*CW crossing river with horse
(1958)*

*CW and Thai carriers
crossing log bridge (1954)*

The Callaway house in Chiangkham served as a base of sorts for believers like Nai Jan Ta and a place to plan and to explore the mountains in search of tribal villages. Baby Jeni was born in 1951, and while Lois mothered her growing brood of four, C.W. went up the mountains a total of nine trips with a friendly and capable Chinese Christian named Jin Yong Sin who served as interpreter. Each trip was about a week long, made for the purpose of getting acquainted with the tribes, and to search for a place for the Callaways to live among them. C.W. and Jin Yong Sin made a strong and committed team and gave a positive witness for the Lord in the villages. Jin Yong Sin's wife was a Mien woman named Fay Orn. When Lois first met Fay Orn, she assumed that she was Thai since she wore traditional Thai clothing, but her Mien heritage, although hidden under the clothing, would prove to be a serendipitous connection for the Callaways.

One day, the Callaways received word that Jin Yong Sin had contracted a serious illness. Even before there was time to check on his condition, he died within days. "When he got sick, he gave himself an injection. I don't know what kind," Fay Orn said. That was all they knew.

It felt like a very long walk to the cemetery in the forest as they carried Jin Yong Sin's body. His body was small and light, but their burden of grief was made heavier by the loss of their hopes of an evangelistic team and dreams of ministry together. The stone in their throats kept them walking in silence and private grief. Jin Yong Sin died leaving his wife with a six-month-old son and his twelve-year-old nephew to raise.

It was the height of the monsoon season when Jin Yong Sin was buried. Fay Orn grieved deeply and wanted to go back to her Mien village to live with her mother. Torrential rains and swollen streams blocked her way. She came to Lois quietly one day and shared her tears. The Callaways drew her into their care and invited her to live with them until she was able to return to her mother. Fay Orn became their first Mien language teacher. The Callaways helped Fay Orn get a small store space in Chiangkham and taught her daily from the Word. Fay Orn and her nephew, Guang were baptized in a river near their home village of Ban Ngao on July 2, 1951. She was the only Mien Christian they knew of, and now, perhaps with her help, there would be many more.

When the monsoon floods finally subsided, Fay Orn went up to her mother's tribal village, Tzan Fu Nyei Laangz. Translated, it means "The Village of Tzan Fu." Lois fondly referred to it as "Tzanfuville." Tzan Fu was the headman of the village and was a cousin to Fay Orn's mother. As was the custom, the extended family often stayed under one roof, and Fay Orn's mother lived with Tzan Fu. As she settled into village life again, Fay Orn told Tzan Fu how the Callaways had befriended her, and that they were in search of a place to live among the Mien. Fay Orn asked him the favor of allowing the foreigners to stay in their village.

Weeks passed. Fay Orn finally came to visit the Callaways again in Chiangkham. Lois could hardly contain herself to ask about the possibility of them moving to Tzanfuville.

"Did Tzan Fu say foreigners could stay in the village?"

"They are frightened of you," Fay Orn said in Chinese.

Only slightly discouraged Lois offered, "Tell them we mean no harm."

"Yes," she said, "They see how your kindness has helped me, but still they are afraid. I will keep trying."

The Mien understood only that the Callaways were strange, huge, white people whose motivations for friendship were unknown. They staunchly believed that all westerners were cannibals. Fay Orn laid the first frail underpinnings of trust for the Callaways. She spoke about their kindness and the many opportunities they had to eat her, and they did not. Tzan Fu and the village elders finally decided it was worth the risk to let them live in their midst. They offered them a site to build a house at the edge of their village, near the ceremonial cremation grounds. Fay Orn brought them the good news.

When the Callaways first heard that there might be a place to stay and minister in Tzanfuville, they immediately made arrangements to scout out their future home. They packed their bags, hired some porters, and wrapped up four-month old Jeni, cooing happily in her baby basket. Lelan, Mark and Joyce stayed in Chiangkham with Imogene and Nurse Dorothy. They covered Jeni's basket with a special net designed to protect her from mosquitoes and big hairy, green caterpillars which occasionally dropped from the trees. The net also served to protect her from the curious, poking fingers of tribal people. Jeni rode suspended on one end of a bamboo pole carried by an older Thai porter whom they were sure would be careful with such precious cargo. On the other end of the pole was a bamboo basket of cloth diapers, baby powder, and diaper pins. Often as the porter rounded an especially steep and sharp curve in the trail, the basket dangled from his long shoulder pole over the edge of a steep cliff. Nothing but miles of sky between the sweet baby and the hard earth below. After a few scares, Lois occasionally opted to walk in front of the porter or to look away, and kept on praying.

The journey took them first through lowland Thai country. They slept on the sleeping porches of the headmen of several Thai villages along the route. The next two or three more nights they found hospitality on the high ridges of the range that marked the border between Laos and North Thailand. They slept on bamboo guest shelves in Hmong homes, grateful for the indoor smoky guest fire that helped keep the mosquitoes away.

Lois holding four-month-old Jeni
in Hmong village (1951)

The Hmong tribal women were particularly excited about Jeni, the first white baby they had ever seen. As they approached the Hmong villages, the women often came clamoring down the trail and begged Lois to take the baby out from under the mosquito net and nurse her. If it wasn't close to her feeding time, Jeni was quickly and noisily passed from woman to woman, gurgling and cooing and often imitating their delighted squeals.

One day they met four Hmong men on the trail. Although these men had traveled a long distance from home, they were turning back because of a bad omen - they had just seen a snake cross the trail before them.

"Where are you going?" they asked, using the standard polite conversation starter.

"We are going to Tzanfuville," C.W. replied.

"What are you going there for?" they asked, using the accepted polite response. It was good that Lois had not yet learned to say, "None of your business." She smiled to herself.

"We have come to tell the people about Jesus."

"Who is Jesus?"

Who is Jesus? They didn't know her Best Friend. These were the nameless and faceless masses that Lois imagined when she read the call in Scripture to preach to "those who have not heard" the name of Christ proclaimed. They stood before her now, no longer faceless, with searching eyes.

"Jesus is God's Son who came down from heaven to save us," C.W. explained as simply as possible. Nothing could have prepared them for the next question.

"Did you come down from heaven too?"

Lois hoped that the utter amazement did not show on her face as she contemplated their question. "No, we are people like you." She could tell in their eyes that the farmers did not believe what they said. As they moved on, she looked back to see them still staring. In what ways could they appear to be people like them? Not many. They were tall, white-skinned with large noses, and had light colored eyes, and their mouths uttered the oddest things.

"You have yellow eyes," Lois was once told by an old Asian woman.

"I would say they were blue or maybe green, but not yellow," Lois said.

"Oh yes," she replied, "They are definitely yellow. You know, we have always been told that demons have yellow eyes." Their physical appearance was the first formidable obstacle in winning the villagers' trust, which was won out slowly. Like the rhythmic motion of the river pushing onto the shore and smoothing the rocks it touches, eventually the sharp edges of mistrust were worn down. For 35 years, the Callaways tediously polished, and eventually God showed them a reflection of Himself in the work.

Chapter 4

Boy Soldier

T he hills of Laos were now a war zone. Yoon Choy carried a gun that was as long as he was tall, and nearly as wide. Some of the adults laughed, "So small. His gun touches to the ground." He received the equivalent of one dollar per month for his services.

Yoon Choy learned how to dodge the gunfire and to dig a hole for himself before he sat down to rest. He learned to keep a good distance from the echoing explosions so that he would always have a course of escape. He ate whatever the earth provided. Sometimes he found a watercress-like plant to eat with his rice, or he hacked away at the thick trunk of the banana tree to boil and eat the tender center. He wished it could have been sweet like the banana, but no.

"Terrible. No taste. Nothing can compare."

When there was fighting, he chewed dry rice.

"I did ambush and spy on the enemy. Sometimes you get killed on the way."

There was a lot of marching. When the United States airplanes dropped water for them, they marched to fetch it. When it was time to get into strategic position, they marched and entrenched themselves. When it was time to get a good vantage point, they marched up the steep mountainside to the tallest peak.

Sleeping was a major task. Dig a hole. The longer they stayed, the deeper the hole. Cut the wood with an axe to cover the hole.

Take turns sleeping at night. The worst part was waking up to the leeches; leeches stuck to his eyes and mouth and around his nose; sometimes covering his face. They were small, black and tapered, about an inch long. If there was any moisture on the ground, there was always the chance of waking up to their detestable slimy bodies invading his face. The trouble was, the enemy knew the fighter planes couldn't fly during the wet, rainy monsoon season in April and May, so that's when they were sent out to fight, stuck with their faces to the wet ground. The leeches thrived in the wetness when hand-to-hand combat was its fiercest. Yoon Choy shivered to a queasy sleep each night in the midst of the fighting, the killing, and the leeches.

Waiting for the enemy was often the hardest. Hunkered down in a deep, wet hole, Yoon Choy's tired mind drifted easily back to the past and the echoes of laughter of the village to escape the present. Catch two male horned beetles. Catch the female. Tie each of the males to the end of a string and a stick. Tie it tight, but don't squish them. Cut a small hole in the middle of a bamboo stick and tie the female inside the hollow center. Gather around! Gather around! Which male beetle will get through the hole first? Who will win? Place your bets! Yoon Choy smiled.

A loud smack of a hard object on the wood above his head brought Yoon Choy back. He heard something rolling around above the hole that he shared with two other soldiers. Something fell between the cracks. He held his breath. He recalled thinking that it was probably some sort of explosive device. Blackness.

Yoon Choy and two others were hit when a bomb found its way through the cracks in the wood that covered their hole. Miraculously they lived. They waited for a night and a day— "not long" for the American Airplane to pick them up. When Yoon Choy stood up he felt blood come down his face, reached up to touch it, and fell down. "I pass out." After recovering from his head injury, he was back fighting again.

Yoon Choy was compelled to join the army so that his older brother could stay back with his mother and help care for the family. He actually met General Vang Pao, the dedicated Hmong leader who first saw combat with the French at the age of thirteen.

General Vang Pao petitioned the Mien for their help in the war to fight for their freedom against the communists. He promised food and money in exchange for the willingness to fight. The Hmong had rallied under the diminutive general. Secretly aided by the American government who could not resist the choice strategic location of Laos to North Vietnam, the C.I.A. had found their manpower.[2] But Vang Pao's people were being destroyed. It has been reported that by 1968, the Silent War, or the "war that wasn't" or "The Other Theater" as it was referred to by those who lived it, had decimated the Hmong. An American pilot described it in calculated terms: "A short time ago we rounded up three hundred fresh recruits. Thirty percent were fourteen years old or less, and ten of them were only ten years old. Another thirty percent were fifteen or sixteen. The remaining forty percent were forty-five or over. Where were the ages in between? I'll tell you—they're all dead."[3] When Yoon Choy joined the secret forces of the C.I.A., he was twelve years old.

Chapter 5

Tzanfuville

Tzanfuville (1958)

When Lois and C.W. found their way to Tzanfuville, a crowd had already gathered. Small groups of turbaned women in their intricately cross-stitched trousers and black coats with furry red yarn neckpieces appeared. Their husbands wore black trousers and shirts with silver buttons, and black skullcaps. Some chatted with the missionaries in Chinese, some told the porters where to put the baskets full of food, clothing, bedding, tracts, and teaching materials. In the background, there was a buzz of discussion in

Mien about the strangers; questions and theories flew wildly about.

Tzan Fu, the village headman came out to greet them. He looked much younger than his thirty years. Surprisingly, he wore casual western clothing. Tzan Fu had learned to read some Chinese as a young boy, and it was clear to Lois that his quick thinking would make him a success in any culture. She imagined for a moment Tzan Fu surrounded in the high dark wood paneled walls of higher learning in the West. She knew he would have scored well above average in any intelligence test; why not, she thought.

The missionaries were welcomed into Tzan Fu's house. As they entered, Lois noticed an ingenious running water system using the clean waters of a mountain spring and a gravity powered network of bamboo pipes attached to the homes. They walked on a hard clay floor. Walls were made of vertical boards topped with an ingenious bamboo tile roof. It was dark; there were no windows and the doors were kept closed to keep the pigs from wandering in. A smoky fire was burning in one corner and four or five men were sitting on low stools smoking a long, gurgling water pipe. A small wrinkled grandmother was squatting on the ground, looking up at the foreigners from her fine embroidery work. Lois smiled. The grandmother smiled back. No teeth. On the far wall was an ancestral altar. A small shelf set about six feet off the ground was displayed with offerings of food, and tea or some sort of liquid, Lois couldn't tell exactly what, in small porcelain cups. One corner of the room was reserved as a guestroom. The Callaways slept there for a few nights, sometimes competing for space with opium smokers.

C.W. sat down and brought out a flannelgraph and tried to give a gospel story in broken Mien and Chinese. Since there was no devil worship in progress, he had the undivided attention of the village. Lois studied the man sitting on the far side of the fire. His eyes were cold and unfocused with opium, and his mouth was deeply lined in a permanent scowl. There was an ominous aura about this man. This was the village demon priest, and former headman, Saeng Meng.

After the story, Lois watched two of Tzan Fu's daughters go through their chores. The eldest was grinding corn on a stone mill. The other stood by the water trough and dipped water into a big pot full of chopped banana trees and special weeds that were boiled up to feed the pigs. The pigs deserved special care at all times for they were kept for demon worship and sacrifice. Lois found that certain nuances in the language could lead one to believe that a mother might be unclear about the exact number of children she had, but was very certain about the number of pigs she had.

Lois sat on the ground peering out into the twilight as the shadows of the jungle deepened. She watched the Mien women silhouetted against the evening sky, trudging up the steep mountain slope bearing on their backs the heavy loads of produce from their fields, some carried a baby strapped to their front swinging with the rhythm of their steps. Lois pulled out an old worn notebook to write.

> To walk the labored path without Him!
> To know no comfort from the Lord;
> To have no hope of peace or blessing;
> To neither know nor love the Word.

Several of the village children gathered around her to see the foreign pencil and the foreign scribblings. Mothers kept a sideways gaze on their children for fear the high nosed one might snatch their child away for a snack.

> To fear both day and night without Him;
> To know no healing at His hand;
> To know no path within the Valley,
> No Shepherd in the barren land.
> To know not of His ruling presence;
> O'ercoming all life's fear and woe;
> To know not of the love of Jesus,
> Who stands triumphant o'er the foe.
> O, when shall come the rising Day Star'
> To shed His light in darkened heart?
> Yes, then they'll know my heart's full burden
> That often makes the teardrops start.

To walk the upward trail beside Him;
To know sweet comfort from the Lord;
To know they've found that peace and blessing
Sweet fellowship within His Word.
To see them claiming peace at evening;
To rise and face the day secure;
To see them shoulder yet the burden,
Yet find His strength that will endure.
To see them in His mighty Presence,
Victorious over death and woe!
Ah this, ah this is grace sufficient
To make me know why He said,"Go!"

Lois eventually became friends with one of the Mien women named M'Lou. Warm and kind, M'Lou had a forthright penchant for the latest gossip. It was from M'Lou that she found what burdensome discussions preceded their welcome by Tzan Fu and the elders into the village. More than just being suspected yellow-eyed demons, their words and assertions about a loving God needed to be tested. Lois' bold assertion that she was not afraid of demons or ghosts had frightened many of the villagers. The demons should not be angered by such arrogance.

The plot of land where they were allowed to build their house was foul-smelling during cremations. The Mien considered the land more than just undesirable, however, it was deemed dangerous and foolish to live on.

"Put them next to the cremation grounds," an elder had suggested, "If they are not afraid of the demons that walk the grounds, then they can stay."

Often Mien mothers, in an effort to fool the spirits, made disparaging remarks about their own children "This is my daughter, the ugly one," so that the spirits would not find them worthy of their attention.

Lois' first Mien home was made of bamboo. When the decision had been made to move to Tzanfuville, she anxiously looked forward to the day where she could settle into a real home for her family. There were lessons to teach and translation work to be done.

She had seen the Mien tribal men at work building a new house, and knew them to be skilled workers. Wielding the huge, heavy hoes which were made by local blacksmiths, they chopped into the foot of a hill to make a perpendicular wedge where they would find clay of a good consistency. Several men dragged away the excess topsoil and clay by pulling split boards and let it all roll down the mountain. A firm clay floor was achieved in this manner. The clay was soaked with water and allowed to dry to a hard smooth surface. Then they were ready to build.

The Callaway's Mien home was a different matter. The area that Tzan Fu had marked out for the house was on a level spot at the foot of the village. There was no hill to slice away to expose the beginnings of a hard clay floor. The floor was made of loose dirt. Water only turned it into mud, so it was useless to try to achieve the hard-packed clay floor such as the Mien had. Most of the houses in the village were made of boards split with an axe and set vertically. A solid roof of bamboo tiles secured on a sturdy frame of girders kept the rain out. The bamboo was dragged in from the surrounding jungle by hand. It was long hard work, but it didn't take long with the willing hands of the extended Mien family. As the Callaways had no extended family to help them build, C.W. asked several Mien men to help build the house. He was met with polite refusals, and no explanation why. The Mien were hard working subsistence farmers. When it was time for field clearing and planting of corn and rice, the men hoed the rough soil for their fields, and wielded the heavy dibble stick which they thrust into the ground again and again to make holes for their wives who followed behind, dropping the rice seed or corn kernels into each hole. Everyone worked, or no one would eat; no rice for family, no corn for pigs and horses. Once the crops were planted, however, the men of the village seemed to have a lot of leisure time. The women continued with the maintenance work of hoeing and weeding. Lois eyed the men sitting together and wondered at their reticence to help them work. They were paying rather generous wages, yet the Mien continued to be politely silent whenever the house subject came up.

Once again, it was M'Lou who finally explained the Mien system to Lois.

"Anyone who works as a day laborer considers himself a slave of the employer for life," she said.

"For life?"

"Yes, and the employer in turn obligates himself to care for that person the rest of his life."

"For life," Lois said, turning over the possible outcomes in her mind, if anyone had indeed responded.

M'Lou continued, "If he does not have a wife, then the employer must furnish the bride price to get him a wife. If he is ill, all doctor bills rightfully come to the employer."

Lois looked gratefully at M'Lou. M'Lou had an intuition of what it felt like to be in a new culture. Lois was glad to be armed with this knowledge when much later, young men who were unable to supply the bride price for the girl of their choice, came to the missionaries and said, "We want to enter you. We will work for you." If not for M'Lou, Lois knew they would have most certainly purchased many, many new daughters-in-law.

Not surprisingly, the Callaways found no one willing to become their slave for life, no matter what the pay. But they still needed a house. In the end, Thai laborers were hired to make the two-day trek up the mountain to build the house. The Thai builders were skillful craftsmen. Their lowland homes, a bit different than the Mien mountain homes, were made with large, heavy bamboo pieces that were flattened into boards for sidewalls, doors and shutters, and topped with a roof of thatched grass. The missionaries were aware that the Thai knew nothing about building mountain homes, but since they knew even less, they licked their wounds of insecurity and proceeded to have them build. *"Kay sah muh she boo,"* it will be fine, Lois thought.

Chapter 6

Bamboo House

Anew home for Lois. The land was cleared and building started in earnest. In preparation for building, the Thai method called for soaking the bamboo for several days in a stream. There was no nearby stream on the mountain to soak their bamboo, but the builders assured Lois that all would be fine. She wondered only for a moment why the soaking process was necessary on the lowlands but not in the mountains. Not that it would matter much, Lois reminded herself that this bamboo house would only be a temporary home, since they were due to leave for furlough in just two years. The builders gathered the grass, which grew abundantly on the hillsides for the roof thatching. Splitting a special type of bamboo into thin slivers, they made a string with which they tied the grass to a long stick of bamboo. This made strips of thatch about four feet long and eighteen inches wide. The bamboo string was then used to tie the strips of thatch to the roofing girders. The roof was said to withstand the elements well and be in good condition for a full year, and with a little ingenious patching, usable under ordinary weather conditions for two or three years. Trying to save time and money, the missionaries decided to give the roof a try on their own. Things looked good, but after comparing their home to those in the lowlands, they realized that they didn't use enough thatch. Their roof didn't look quite as substantial as their lowland neighbors. *"Kay sah muh she boo."* They saved time and money by using only a four-inch overlap. It was only meant to be a temporary house after all, and so they proceeded with the building.

It wasn't long after they had settled into their new bamboo house that the missionaries found out why the Thai soaked the bamboo in water before building. The soaking process killed the multitudinous clusters of insect eggs that infested the wood. As they hatched, the bugs feasted on the walls of Lois' new home, and as they multiplied, they feasted even more. Although the house was still standing, this left a fine dust on everything as the bugs pulverized the walls, and caused tiny cracks to widen, making it very convenient for curious eyes to peek through. Once, when the children were battling uncomfortable and seemingly uncontrollable sandfly ulcers, Nurse Dorothy teased Lois about her "airy" home, saying that the children were in an optimal situation since her medical book said the best control of the pests was ample ventilation.

The layout of the house was almost tribal. There was a bamboo door at each end of the room which made it highly accessible to the neighbors, their children, their dogs, and an occasional stray pig. Near the center of the room was a cast iron tripod. This sat atop a log fire, which burned and smoked intermittently throughout the day. Lois boiled water over the fire for their own potable water supply, and kept a kettle ready to make a welcoming cup of tea. Small wicker stools and a few wooden stools provided tribal style seating for the frequent guests. Putting a cast iron Dutch oven on the tripod allowed Lois to bake bread for her family of six, and cook the meals which consisted mostly of rice and vegetables, meat of some sort, and occasionally, sausage.

At one end of the commons room, which was about forty feet long and twenty feet wide, there was a hollowed out log which served as a water tank. It caught the water, which ran from a four-inch bamboo pipe. Tzan Fu kindly let the Callaways hook into his water line. The water source was a spring a quarter of a mile or so above the village on the side of the mountain. The water came down to the house via bamboo pipes resting in forked posts set firmly in the ground. Lois learned to ration water, and taught the boys to help in the upkeep of the water line when pigs or horses knocked the pipes over, or if they filled up with falling leaves and lichen.

"Showers" were taken around this log water tank. Lois learned to wear a sarong to bathe, dipped water from the tank, and poured it over herself. Sometimes guests milled around as the family bathed, undaunted by what used to be a rather private moment.

It was because of the water line that Lois first recognized she had an enemy in the village. Often where no horse would ever venture, the line was mysteriously diverted. On laundry day, as Lois started filling her "washing machine," the water supply would trickle down to nothing. All evidence pointed to Tzan Fu's mother, the smiling old lady with the large gaps between her gold teeth. Lois referred to her, often through clenched jaws, as "The Matriarch." In the village, the Matriarch was known as "Granny Bet." Lois made Granny Bet an object of relentless prayer, channeling her anger through hands clenched in petition, and a compliant heart.

One full side of the house was the semi-private living quarters. The room ran parallel to the commons. A partition enclosed the dining room and kitchen area, about twelve feet by twelve feet. Above the folding table was a big picture window covered in plastic that framed a glorious view. Majestic trees, cloud capped mountain peaks and when the clouds lifted, Lois could see the beautiful Mekong River, a steel blue ribbon far in the distance, which from that point north was the border between Thailand and Laos.

All their belongings were packed and hauled two days by oxcart to the base of the mountain, then carried by porters and horses five-hours to their bamboo home. Food supplies were stashed in what Lois called "bomb lockers," which were sturdy olive green, government surplus wooden boxes. Once inside the house, they were turned on end to make cupboards.

The other end of the living quarters was more private and accessible only from the dining area. The mattresses were laid on the floor and covered by mosquito nets. Clothing was stashed in suitcases and rat-proof lockers, which were nailed to the inside partition wall. Two other rooms were on the other side of the house, a guest room with a sleeping shelf for guests, and an area for storage.

Out of necessity, the storage room was eventually converted to an opium addicts' cure room. Several Mien men came to the Callaways wanting to take the cure. When the debilitating withdrawal symptoms set in, the responses varied. Some simply got up and left, others arranged for family to deliver their opium to them through the outside wall. Years later, C.W. and Lois and co-workers recognized the spiritual component to this problem and only accepted patients for the opium cure who were making a commitment to Jesus. With these committed Christians, they then realized an 80% cure rate. A doctor who worked in a government substance abuse hospital at the time reported only a 10% cure rate.

Lois wih Mien friends
(1952)

Touring the newly built bamboo house, M'Lou was quick to point out that there were more than a few Mien amenities lacking. There was no rice pounder for the daily milling of the rice for the family. Their rice had to be hauled up in horse pack loads from rice mills at the foot of the mountain. Lois had no huge wok for boiling pig food for her pigs. Their pigs ate only raw food, and were rather pitied in the village. Neither did she have a neatly cut two-hole fireplace that could hold two ordinary sized woks or one wok and a cast iron rice pot. Lois felt the pity by M'Lou and her Mien neighbors; cooking on a campfire, just like a traveler on the trail. "*Kay sah muh she boo.*" It was temporary after all.

At any rate, Lois had work to do. She loved her kids. She taught them how to read. She taught villagers the Word of God. She baked bread and she fried up sausages over an open fire, just like her grandmother taught her back in Colorado - except for the open fire part. And when she made sausages, C.W. had to slaughter a whole pig first. Lois would stoke the fire, scald the pig parts, and eventually get to stripping down the intestinal lining and stuffing them with seasonings and meat, twisting off at intervals and then frying down the sausage and lard. She was an ocean away from her apron-starched American counterparts, (she still wore an apron, but the starch would have been a waste in the humid jungle climate), yet she was just like them; an All-American Mom in Thailand, in a drafty bamboo hut. Sausages. One lanky Texan. Four little babies (and one more on the way). New languages. New faith. New friends. This was Lois Callaway's life.

Lois and Joyce in Mien clothing (1954)

During the summer months wonderful interactions took place in the commons room. It was like a great social hall and place of education for the Mien, many of whom in those days, had never even been down the mountain to visit a lowland Thai village.

On the other side of the commons room was a ten by ten foot area used for home schooling. Desks were made of bomb lockers. Both Lelan and Mark were being homeschooled by Lois, and Joyce was eager to get started with kindergarten. The schoolroom had a loosely locked door for privacy, which Lois often reluctantly opened for the constant flow of curious visitors.

One day, during lesson time, the Matriarch came to visit Lois carrying her two-year-old grandchild on her back. She yelled and insisted that Lois go to the commons room to play the organ for her. The Matriarch was a sharp-tongued woman, the most feared in the village because of her social position within the tribe. She had been very friendly to Lois when there was some material gain for herself, but that was all. Out of respect to her, the Callaways called her "Granny Bet," but it took prayer and strength to do even that much.

"Come play the organ now," she yelled behind the closed door. Lois bristled at her tone.

Lois called out loudly and deliberately, "I am very busy teaching my children."

The Matriarch countered, "But my granddaughter wants to hear the organ." Determined not to interrupt Lelan's class, Lois did the unthinkable. She kept the Matriarch waiting outside for a full five minutes.

Her demands persisted. "My granddaughter wants to hear the organ now." Lois knew it would take less time to go play a couple of tunes for the Matriarch than to argue the value of her time.

"I'll be right back," she whispered to Lelan.

The Matriarch enjoyed a simple concert, and was an appreciative audience. Lois silently wondered about the hardness of the Matriarch's heart, and when she finished, she took a bow, and returned to teaching Lelan in the next room.

Through their long stay in the bamboo house, the Callaways had proved to the villagers that they were not afraid of the demons. The Callaways apparently passed the test, the demons did not bother them, but Lois faced her own demons each morning. Pregnant with her fifth baby, each new morning brought waves of nausea. Lois stayed in her new home even as the wind blew the stench of cremation through the cracks. The Mien saw that the missionaries were very serious about living with them. Although they spoke strangely and looked so pale and awkwardly tall, they did freely give out medicine and told interesting stories. The Callaways gained a little respect and slowly the villagers came to see them as a part of their village.

Lois lost twenty-five pounds from the morning sickness and fumes from the cremation grounds. After a year in the bamboo house, they endured the tail of a hurricane, which left the already thinned grass roof in shreds. Shredded thatch dropped into cereal bowls and hair. Rain dripped into their soup through the gaps in the thatch. Colorful plastic sheets were draped over the dining table, school desks and beds, tent style. M'Lou told Lois that the villagers pitied them that they should live in such a poorly built house. By November, with cold winds blowing across the mountain slopes and whistling through the cracks - and a baby due in about three months - it was time to abandon the disposable bamboo home. So the Callaways temporarily left, making the slow trek down the mountain to a rental home on the Thai plains.

Chapter 7

Cabin in the Clouds

Enduring intense morning sickness during her pregnancy, exacerbated by the pungent smells of the cremation grounds, Lois was rewarded with her fifth child. Joel David was born in Chiangkham, Thailand on February 17, 1953. Welcoming him into the world were the gentle hands of Nurse Dorothy, and Imogene Williams. Shortly after David's birth, the Callaways departed for the United States on furlough, once again with a bottom to diaper between countries.

They returned to a new President, Dwight D. Eisenhower and Vice-President, Richard M. Nixon. The Callaways moved into a small, drafty apartment and enrolled in classes at the Wycliffe Bible Translators Summer Institute of Linguistics in Norman, Oklahoma. There they gained skills for learning an unwritten language and developing an alphabet. Lois received new insights into cross-cultural living and communication. After a year of studies and shuffling bodies around in the crowded apartment, she had sufficiently recovered from her pre-furlough bout of American nostalgia, and was ready to return to her mission field in Thailand, her little Mien village of Tzanfuville. Plans for a new home were in the making, and she couldn't wait to go back.

This time the Mien afforded the Callaways more leeway in choosing the site for their home. A good distance from the cremation grounds was Lois' first thought. They decided upon a site along the trail to the fields where the Mien worked daily. There they would be very much in the mainstream of everyday Mien life.

There were two basic needs for the new home. It had to be substantial enough to survive wind and rain, and it had to afford privacy. This second need was of the utmost importance as the children were now older and needed to have time away from prying eyes. The floor plan included an office, kitchen, and clinic, a second story for the bedrooms and living room, and an attic.

Plans in hand, they were ready to build. C.W. found Thai workers to fell and cut trees into boards of various sizes, and a carpenter willing to work in a tribal village long enough to finish the work. They had no funds in hand to pay for this labor, and had to ask the Lord to provide, and He did. C.W. spent half of his time for the next year in Tzanfuville, supervising, cajoling and paying the workers. He used his time in the village to continue the teaching that had begun when they lived in the bamboo house. Lois remained in the mission home in Chiangkham, homeschooling Lelan and Mark and teaching in the Thai villages. Finding herself alone with the children, her job was clear; be a mother, be a teacher. Mother Teacher had to care for four measle-ridden children at once and yet continued teaching. It was a very effective weight loss program, she claimed, but she emphatically preferred other means.

When C.W. returned periodically from Tzanfuville, he would update Lois on the progress of their "Cabin in the Clouds," as they came to call it. Lois was quite dismayed when she heard that the lumber they used was never dried and seasoned. This meant that as the lumber dried, it would warp and create yet another drafty, open-for-public-inspection home. Ah well, *"Kay sah muh she boo."*

It had been fifteen months since they returned from furlough, but it felt much longer. The "Cabin in the Clouds" was finally finished with a fine roof of aluminum sheeting. The move had to be made soon or the monsoon-swollen rivers would make the trails impassable. A break in the weather gave two days of reasonably dry roads to make the move. Oxcarts were loaded with the mattresses, crates of supplies, clothing, books, and teaching materials all packed in the green army bomb lockers. The children loved the trip.

Lelan and Mark helped to drive the oxen and dreamed of the day they would own their own oxcarts. Joyce, Jeni and David enjoyed the bumpy oxcart ride. When the road was wide enough, the children were occasionally allowed to run alongside. C.W. supervised the whole operation, and Lois, who had vowed never to ride in an oxcart as long as she was able-bodied and of sound mind, surrendered to exhaustion from the days of preparation and teaching and mothering, and lay down on one of the mattresses in an oxcart and slept most of the two day trip to the foot of the hills. By then Lois was refreshed and ready to face the steep, five-hour hike up the mountain.

Callaway family in their
mountain home (1955)

It was good to be home. They passed the Mien homes on the winding trail up to their new home. They stopped in to visit a few friends along the way. Entering from the bright sunlight, they blinked and waited until their eyes adjusted to the darkness inside. Close to mealtime, the women were moving about the small smoky fire burning in the corner of the house. The men sat conversing around the fire, passing the ancient Chinese water pipe back and forth between words.

M'Lou smiled at Lois, "Where have you been? We have watched the days, and watched the days but never saw you at the trail's horizon." They chatted for a while and then the family made their way up the rest of the trail to the house perched like a castle, on the lovely mountainside.

A large flat area had been cleared in front of the house for recreation. The children ran about. C.W. had to explain to many villagers that he was not making an airstrip for plane landings, just a place to play badminton, which also had to be explained. The war that wasn't supposed to be; the Silent War that no one in America talked about, and the president denied, was happening next door in Laos. The villagers were made very aware of warfare activity, and the need for airstrips.

Callaway family at their
mountain home (1960)

All seven Callaways entered the large room, the temporary dining room and clinic. Also on the first floor: C.W.'s office, and the kitchen. A short, steep flight of stairs led to a landing with a closed, but not locked door, which led to yet another flight of stairs. There was a larger room that would be their future dining room, and around the bend were the sleeping quarters. A little sitting room partitioned off by the attic stairs, was complete with a homey wood stove and built in "sofa" which Lois eventually covered with a mattress and flowered chintz. Another steep flight of stairs wound past a landing and up to the attic.

Quickly they filled the bookcase with books, organized the bomb locker desks and hung the mosquito nets over the beds. The carpenters had made the beds of roughly hewn timber. In the kitchen, they set up the cast iron sheepherder's stove. No more cooking over an open fire. In the sitting room, they mounted three bomb lockers to be used as the children's desks, with the bottom resting against the wall and the lid falling open on the front side. A piece of chain attached to the lid allowed the lid to drop down to form a desktop that could be closed when homework was finished. Lelan was in the fifth grade, and Mark in second. Eventually the other children too started home schooling.

They later found that the winding stairs with the landing and door intimidated all but the bravest Mien from access to the schoolroom. This was just the privacy the children needed to complete their lessons. It was no deterrent, however, to one of Lelan's friends, the twelve-year-old son of Tzan Fu, whom they affectionately called, "Inquisitive" or "Inquiz." When Lois returned home one day from an emergency medical visit, she found that this young man had dug his toes into the clapboard walls of the house and scaled the wall. He chatted with Lelan as he was hanging from the window. Sensing trouble as he saw Lois approaching, he quickly shinnied down the wall and disappeared into the surrounding jungle.

A shelf in the corner of the dining room held a phonograph which they used to entertain and teach the guests. Another was mounted at shoulder level and stored the supply of aspirin, vitamins, antihistamines, malaria medicine, diarrhea potion, first aid equipment, and the village's only stethoscope. Tzanfuville was a hard two-day walk to the nearest medical doctor, so the Callaways were able to meet a great need for the villagers.

After a long day of travel and unpacking, early the next morning, two villagers stopped by the new clinic for medicine on their way to the fields. Then at sundown, several Mien came back up the trails with the produce from their fields in back-baskets, hoping to trade their produce for lumps of brown sugar, flashlight batteries, kerosene, or more medicine.

Each morning Lois greeted the villagers and their assortment of maladies. She slept soundly each night. This night, however, was different. Lois awoke suddenly to a blast of the ram's horn. She knew what this meant. Death. In the darkness Lois heard a loud shrill wail of an older woman. Granny Bet. The rain pounded on the thin aluminum roof with increased intensity, and the roll of thunder ended in an earsplitting clap that momentarily shut out the sound of her wailing. The reverberating sound of the second blast on the ram's horn made an eerie symphony with the rain pounding her roof and splattering upon the broad, heavy foliage of the rain forest about the village.

Lois pondered as she waited for the third and final blast of the trumpet. In the house on the ridge just above them Lois pictured Granny's small frame crumpled and weeping. Gramps had been very ill for a long time, though he scarcely knew it. Any discomfort had long ago been deadened and distorted into the haze of his opium pipe. The heavy, penetrating odor of the opium was sweet, but once inhaled, the tendrils of smoke infused into his family and brought only bitterness and increasing poverty. He was once quite wealthy, and although in the end, his family was impoverished though his addiction, he was not begrudged. At least one pipe of opium per day was budgeted and stashed each year during the January opium harvest for Gramp's daily euphoria.

The third blast cut through her thoughts for a moment. A lull in the rain opened a channel for Granny's wails. Her cries intensified as her grandchildren joined her in a discordant dirge of mourning. Lois moved to her window as the frenetic beat of the drums embedded itself in the roar of jungle rain. The rattling bursts of thunder accented the incessant drumbeat. Lois got up from her bed and looked out into the darkness. Magnificent flashes of lightning illumined the movement of the mourning family like an unearthly strobe.

As the sky slowly brightened in the new dawn light, Lois knew the women of the house would be beginning the preparation for the funeral feast. The noisy rain subsided. She could hear the monstrous thud, thud, thud of the rice pounder. It was probably

Muang, Lois thought, the oldest daughter-in-law, who began the rice preparation. All morning many of the girls of the family vented their grief as they stomped at one end of the long teeter-totter-like pole of the rice pounder. As they stepped down, it lifted the pounding end out of the hollowed out log that contained the unhulled rice. Stepping off, the heavy pounding end smashed down into the grain. On again. Off again. On again. Off again. Thump. Thump. Thump. Then, with a winnowing tray and a sweeping rhythmic motion, the hulls and bran were whisked away by the fanning of the tray and the whole white grains were caught in mid-air. A bushel of rice took two hours to prepare. Mounds and mounds of rice were cooked in huge hollowed out log rice steamers that were set in giant woks.

The drums were now accompanied by the wail of other women who had arrived to help Granny grieve. Soon Lois heard the thud of a great axe. Splitting boards for the casket and the bier, Lois thought as she slowly dressed. The diviners worked to determine the auspicious time when Gramp's wasted body would be carried out of the death door at the back of the house to be cremated in a special area. There was more wailing. Then Lois heard the loud chants of the shamans, more rhythmic drums, the clang of cymbals, and the eerie cry of the wooden flute.

Played in a minor key, all the music of the flute seemed randomly mournful to her uninitiated ear. To the Mien, their well-tuned ears picked out certain cadences that told a melodic story of death, grief, hopelessness and depletion of the family resources.

Lois made a quick breakfast for the children and climbed down the slippery, muddy trail to Granny's house. She heard the shamans call for more hogs to be butchered in sacrifice for Gramp's migrating seven-fold soul. His soul had to find the path to the spirit land of his ancestors, and willingly walk it, otherwise his spirit might stay around the house and fields doing mischief to the family, taking his revenge on everyone for failing to give him a proper send-off.

Gramps was an unusually benevolent man. Being kind was not necessarily a virtue in Mien eyes if it smacked of weakness. Like all other Mien men, he had been dedicated to the spirits at birth with a special request to the godfather spirit that he "make the man-child mean so that he will grow up overcoming all competition and become a strong leader in his tribe." The spirits, it seemed, were very adept at honoring this request in many Mien men, and thankfully less so in others like Gramps.

Lois recognized Granny's voice as she occasionally renewed the wail. If it hadn't been for Gramps' strong adherence to the spirits, Granny might have shown more personal interest in the gospel. And perhaps less animosity toward Lois.

Mien tradition held that a gatekeeper at the river held a book of Gramps' merits. He would then be allowed into the adult section of the Land of the Ancestors. There, Gramps would wait out his time until his reincarnation back to this world. In the meantime, he would farm the hillside fields of the mountain people in the spirit world.

Before Gramps died, each of his sons took turns lifting his head three times each and said, "Go well." The Mien believed this helped a person die peacefully. The family members washed his body, cut his hair and removed gold caps from his teeth.

Tzan Fu closed the eyes of his father and put a tiny piece of silver into his mouth. This gave him an 'expensive mouth'.

"This is so that my father will say only good things and not tell lies," he said.

Six men were chosen by the priest to make the casket. Gramp's casket was decorated with streamers and rice and joss stick offerings were placed on it. Paper money was made, pigs were slaughtered, and plans for a huge feast, to last several days were made in order to placate Gramps in the event that he became a vengeful spirit.

There were countless rituals to be observed in the house. The priest determined the auspicious time for the casket to be taken out of the house to the cremation site. Once on the funeral pyre, a rooster was carried around the casket three times. The rooster is said to possess the soul of Gramps, and was carried back to the village to be set free after three days.

When the funeral pyre was finally lit, and once it was burning with an intense heat, Lois saw everyone returning to the village. The priest was last in line. He turned and squatted, praying that the door of the village will be closed to keep the spirits of the dead from entering. There was still worry that even though all the rules were followed, that Gramps might return at night to appear in dreams. He might be hungry, or he might be telling them there was an error in the ceremony and that would require more offerings and sacrifices to appease his soul.

Lois entered the crowded home and went over to sit with Granny on a tiny wicker stool and held her hand. She remembered how the smoke of the cremation grounds had added so much misery to her morning sickness while she lived in the bamboo house. Now, again, death brought the wave of nauseating sadness.

Chapter 8

Word-Gathering Box

Although Lois maintained a fairly tribal lifestyle, she did have a few modern marvels. Her favorite was her hand-operated washing machine, a square, galvanized iron tub, painted a lovely shade of cream. It was with great amazement that the Mien watched as Lois heated water on the tripod, filled the machine with hot water, put in the clothes, added soap powder, and proceeded to churn the clothes with the handle on the top of the machine. It even had a hand-wringer. Some of the tribal boys enjoyed taking a turn at the handle.

The village favorite (and Granny Bet's) was the small folding pump organ the Callaways had brought from England. The Mien gathered around and stared at the organ, waiting to see where the sounds were created. A funny, likable grandpa came into the commons room one day and wandered around, touching, stroking and looking at every unusual object in the room. The organ was folded down into its box and looked brown and ordinary. He walked past the organ and stopped at the washing machine. Grandpa looked it over carefully, gingerly fingering the handle, and carefully inspecting the ringer from all angles. He turned the handle and found that it produced no sound.

He then called out shyly to Lois, "I'd like to hear this. Would you play it for me, please?"

Unfolding the organ instead, Lois said, "Gramps, I really think you would enjoy this more." She explained that the other was the washing machine and its only sound was splashing water, but music came out of this one. He enjoyed Lois' playing and Lois, a self-proclaimed piano school dropout, mused how her simple concerts were now in such high demand.

The typewriter, or "book beater box" was another awe-inspiring sight for the Mien. When Lois made the box "beat out" Mien words, they were even more amazed. Sometimes she felt sorry for her preliterate friends as they watched with a child-like wonder, the symbols which had no meaning to them. One day, M'Lou said to Lois, "Oh, you can write, even on the book beater box, but..." she lifted her foot on a stool, and pointed to her beautifully embroidered trousers, "...can you do this?" Lois smiled. She couldn't, and suddenly her pity felt misplaced.

"Swei jao lo ma?" came the voice of someone on the back porch. "Are you asleep?" a man had called out in Chinese. Lois knew why he had come. In 1954, the Callaways received their first set of phonograph records of the Gospel messages, and testimonies in the various tribal languages. Since that time, news spread rapidly that the foreign teachers had talking platters that told a story in their own language. Having to hear the words themselves before they dared believe it to be true, they would come at all hours of the day and night; while the missionaries did their language studies, while they ate, and sometimes while they slept. One day, a group of people approached Lois and said, "We hear that you have talking platters. Our parents died many years ago and we want to hear our parents speak to us." The talking platter was a powerful tool, but it often required some explanation to the villagers. Eventually, C.W. hooked the phonograph up to a stationary bicycle then he, Lelan, and Mark spent many hours pedaling the bike to make the platter talk the Gospel in Mien.

It was evident early in the ministry that the Thai often looked down upon the mountain people as below their social standing. An interesting turn of events occurred one day while an ethnically mixed group was gathered around the phonograph. When a recording was played in a tribal language, the Thai could not understand it. The tribal people, obviously pleased with their advantage, smiled and nodded their heads in silent superiority. The Thai grew impatient and sarcastically said, "If you really understand, then tell us what it says."

A Mien villager eventually complied at this point, "The talking platter says 'don't be afraid of evil spirits...it says to believe in Jesus'" and so followed a sermon given by the lowly tribespeople to the Thai.

When the Callaways were able to get a tape recorder that too provided a great attraction for the Mien who promptly named it "the word-gathering box." Those early models without transistors were bulky and required some twenty-four batteries to operate. The word-gathering box preached, and sang, and brought personal messages to those in the tribes from friends and families that lived several days' walk away.

Brother Six (on left) with his wife and granddaughters; Lois (back center) between Mary Baldock and Sylvia Lombard; David, Joyce and Jeni in front center (1958)

"Tzan Fu, ah! Teacher has brought the word-gathering box for me to put some of my words in it to send you. I am Gwei Ching, your very own relative, and I want to urge you to enter Christ as I have done." Gwei Ching, or "Brother Six," as the missionaries called him, was a warm Christian leader. His position as sixth son of his parents was indicated by his other name "Lao Lou." The Mien stood in awe, watching the spindles turn on the old tape recorder, listening intently to the words coming forth from the little plastic box. Lao Lou was a convert from north of Chiang Rai. He sent his urgent witness to his relatives in Tzanfuville. After a little discussion, it was decided that Saeng Meng, the demon priest, would speak for Tzan Fu and the rest of the village.

"Gwei Ching, ah! We were all very glad to hear the words you put in the box for us. There are many questions we have to ask you. We still do not understand how Jesus can protect us from the demons, or if He really will."

Weeks later Gwei Ching listened to Saeng Meng's reply, nodding knowingly. He remembered how he too, at one time wondered how God could love the Mien and how they could be sure of that love. Sympathetically he again gathered his words to the box. "Don't be afraid! Just untie your hearts and let them go. Enter Christ and find out how very much He loves you. When I taste sugar it doesn't sweeten your mouth, but mine only. When I believe in Christ I taste of His strength and love. If you want to know His strength and love, then you too, must taste of Him."

Gwei Ching's response was still met with narrow-eyed skepticism.

Lois once told a Mien woman, "Jesus loves you."

This only brought the reply, "I can see that He loves you. You have five healthy children. You are rich. How can I be sure that Jesus would love the Mien people? We have the spirits and you have yours. No, we can't be sure that Jesus would love and care for us as He obviously does you."

To dispel the generations of fear would be a miracle.

Lois once switched the recorder on while casually conversing with the Mien. She often used their conversations for later language study. When she asked if they'd like to put some of their own words in the box, they were ecstatic. "Could we?" they asked. The answer was to play back for them the words exchanged just a few moments ago.

"Pay fu high, pay fu high."

The words meant "marvelous miracle." She had never heard this phrase before. In all the years of language study, Lois had never found a phrase to translate a marvelous miracle. How frustrating it was to be left without a superlative to describe the wonder of God Himself and His works. As the tape played on, and she listened to their delighted comments, she found herself murmuring with the Mien, *"pay fu high, pay fu high,"* for that is what was needed to change their hearts from fear to trust.

Chapter 9

Mother Teacher

"Those who wait on the Lord shall gain new strength, they shall mount up on wings like a sardine..." This was part of the package deal of going overseas: being linguistically humiliated.

When first in Thailand, Lois needed a language teacher. They finally found a Christian Thai man who was willing to spend some time as their teacher.

The boys, however, spending more and more time with the locals, seemed to have no problem picking up the language. All of it. They were learning through life experience, in context, but Lois didn't know how to weed out the unnecessary filth from the essential vocabulary and grammar. She hardly knew how to ask the time of day. Problem. When she heard silly, mischievous laughter, or angry-toned words that she didn't know, she became increasingly concerned. She decided she would just have to learn those four-letter words in Thai. Lois approached her teacher one day.

"Please tell me the bad words my children say, so that I might teach them properly."

"Oh no," was his reply, "You are a missionary. We are Christians. This will not happen." He firmly set his jaw and looked down at the ground.

"But surely you can see that the children need to be corrected!"

His look softened, then his eyebrows arched in confusion.

"We should not say these words."

Lois managed to compose herself to make a compromise.

"When you hear my children using a foul word, will you please stop them and explain to them why they must not say that?"

"Yes, I can do this."

While he reprimanded, Lois jotted the word down so that she could remember it. It was her personal little black book of bad words.

Little ones would be sent out of the yard time and again shaking their heads in shock, "How could she know that word? She doesn't even speak Thai!" A cursing missionary was beyond their comprehension. Whenever Lois heard one of them using a forbidden word in the fenced in compound, she would lean out the window and say, "Don't say that again, or out you go!" It wasn't long before Lois would hear conversations in the compound that would start with profanity, and end with another child quickly saying, "Yoot, Stop, you'd better not say that word, or she will put you out."

After two years of Central and Northern Thai language and cultural study, Lois could handle simple conversations and felt more confident in conveying spiritual truths. During one trip up the mountain to visit the tribes, their hosts brought food and drink, and repeatedly offered more, probably wondering how they might be able to fill up such large bodies, and were most kind. In return for their kindness, Lois decided that she surely could, with the aid of pictures she had brought along, teach them in their own dialect, about the creation of the world. The people listened well. Lois felt encouraged and excited at her first attempt to communicate the vital Message in a new language.

About three weeks later, Lois' language teacher returned from a trip to that same village. He was laughing. He said, "Those people really did appreciate your story about how Buddha created the world. They had never heard that one before."

Lois was mortified and stammered, "What did I say?"

He explained, "You told them that Pra Jow 'God', had created the earth, but to them, Pra Jow is 'God Buddha'. You should have told them that 'Jehovah God, the Father of Jesus' created the earth. No matter," he said smiling, " I set them straight, but do be careful."

Later in the Mien village, one man who occasionally dropped by the house to ask questions was Saeng Meng, the former headman and demon priest of the village. Lois remembered his was the scowling face behind the smoky fire when she first visited Tzanfuville. Saeng Meng was fairly tall for a Mien man. He stood about 5'10" or more. He seldom smiled. The villagers told Lois he was a murderer, and they were afraid of him. Saeng Meng was an opium addict and smoked his opium pipe three times a day. Though only in his fifties, he was no longer mentally alert, and did not have the capacity to carry on the responsibilities of headman. With so much time on his hands, he would come to sit with Lois in the clinic room and talk in Chinese.

During their early days in the bamboo house, Saeng Meng declared that he would teach the missionaries the Mien language. Help was needed with even the most basic sentences at that point. They were delighted. He gave the Mien names for twenty types of bamboo, excused himself and left. He never gave another Mien language lesson. He did, however, continue to visit and peppered their conversations with questions.

"Where is America?" he asked. "How do you get there? Do you just keep walking over more and more mountains to get there? Do you have the same sun in America that we have here?"

The Callaways invested in a world globe for geography lessons with Saeng Meng. Others in the village too, showed interest in the world beyond their mountains.

"Where did you learn Chinese?" Saeng Meng asked.

"We went to Kunming to learn the Chinese language."

"Why?"

"We wanted to teach the tribespeople along the China-Burma border," C.W. explained, as simply as he could.

Saeng Meng's eyes lit up. "There are Mien up there in that area, in Tali, you know." They didn't know, and wanted to hear more.

"Yes," he continued, "We had a letter from our relatives in that area wanting us to move up to Tali. They tell us that there are many Mien in that area and that they are in charge of the government up there. The soil is so good they can plant enough in one year to feed their families for three years and they want us to join them there."

Lois was perplexed. Investigations of that area had never revealed any Mien there. Having just left China a couple of years before, she also knew it to be an area of civil unrest. Guerrilla warfare was reported all around and tribal Christians were being severely persecuted.

Concerned, she asked, "Are you thinking about moving up there?"

"We are still thinking about it. It does sound like a good place," Saeng Meng replied.

"How long ago did you receive this letter?"

Saeng Meng, in Asian style began counting the cycles of twelve years on the joints of his fingers. Three joints on each of four fingers completed a twelve-year cycle. In a minute or so he replied, "Oh, about seventy years ago, I should say."

Seventy years? At that point, Lois started to understand what the Mien meant when they said, *"Manc-manc, hnamv hnamv, gorngv gorngv."* "Slowly slowly, think think, talk talk." The Mien rarely made a poor decision because of rushing into it.

It took seventy years to slowly, slowly, think and talk about a decision to move to an inviting place like Tali. How long would it take for them to decide to turn from demon worship to Christ? How long before they considered her a person "just like them" and not a demon? No matter how good the Gospel, and no matter how well Lois might master the language, she would still have to wait for them to slowly slowly, think think, talk talk.

Doing her bidding on many occasions, the command performance organ recital being just one incident, Lois and Granny Bet, the Matriarch, eventually became special friends. It must have been all those hand-clenched prayers. When Lois needed a teacher to help her intensify her efforts and progress in learning the Mien language, Granny had come to her aid.

Lois loved Granny's snaggle-toothed smile. In keeping with a cultural beautification ritual, Granny once had thin gold plates anchored around her teeth. Unfortunately, infection set in under each plate. Granny had to daily endure the gnawing agony of rotten teeth and haphazard extractions. She often joined her husband at the opium pipe or chewed a few of his opium dregs throughout the day for relief from the pain. The large gaps between her few healthy teeth had her speaking with a constant lisp. With Granny as Lois' primary language role model, she too started speaking Mien with a Granny-like lisp.

Granny Bet taught Lois far more than lispy Mien words. She taught her the customs and culture of the family.

"Life in the tribe has changed," she lisped ruefully, "The young ones have no respect for the rules of the ancestral spirits. When I was a girl, a full month's penalty was required of mothers of illegitimate babies. They were not allowed to set foot in the family home."

"What is it like now, Granny?" Lois asked.

Granny grimaced, "Families now let girls deliver their illegitimate babies right in the family house. Sometimes they are quarantined for only three days."

Lois often found Granny working on her embroidery while sitting on the short, six-inch bamboo stool. Sometimes she would be making the intricate network of tiny silver bells for her granddaughter's forthcoming wedding. If men were present, she would politely squat nearby, allowing the men to sit on the stools. She had an old decrepit pair of glasses that hung on her small nose, and she squinted as she worked. Granny had the honor of being the oldest person in the village.

"Granny, how old are you?" Lois asked one day.

"Oh, more than seventy," she replied, "I lived over sixty years before I ever saw a white person," she smiled widely showing the gaps in her teeth.

Initial efforts to use the Mien language probably alienated the Mien from the Callaways further than they ever knew. Each linguistic error seemed only to strengthen the Mien's belief about their demon origins. Early attempts at translating evangelical jargon into a language with such a completely different worldview must have confused them even more. As one girl expressed it to Lois years after they first came, "Yes, we thought the way you spoke and wrote our language was a bit strange, but then we supposed that for such a strange new religion there also had to be a strange new language."

Because the Mien had no written language, the Callaways struggled to learn it. There was difficulty in collecting language samples as well. When the Mien found they spoke Chinese, they preferred to speak in their dialect of Chinese. It made language acquisition a slower process, but along the way, they did learn much of their history, legends, and myths. Lois found there were limits to using Chinese, however, especially when talking about spiritual matters. For years, Chinese has been used by the Mien primarily as a trade language to barter for the opium grown in their fields. Spiritual matters were difficult to express using only terms of negotiation.

One day, Lois was listening with her stethoscope to the chest of a lady while her ten-year-old son observed the procedure with fascination. When Lois had meant to say, "Please breathe deeply" the little boy literally rolled onto the floor with laughter, while his mother tried to control her own embarrassed laughter. Lois had mistakenly told her to "get very angry." They all laughed together, and after that, Lois never did confuse the two.

Lois had also been known to say, "The medicine eats father." But it was clear to the Mien what her meaning was. Lois was dispensing freely of all she had, and in the process, her eyes started to lose that yellow glow.

Later Lois learned to share about Jesus quite simply in their own direct and often very expressive words. She knew she had used the proper terminology when one day, a Mien woman said to her, "Oh, He is the Son of our Creator God. You have His Book. We used to have His Book but we ate ours years ago and lost track of Him. Tell me more."

It took two years for Lois to learn to converse and three years to begin to think in Mien. Tzan Fu approached Lois one day, asking if he could help with Bible translations. For four years they had asked for his help. Lois was convinced that this was the man who would best help their cause. He was a patient man. He listened quietly and intently, even as difficult concepts were explained that required gesturing and lengthy, convoluted descriptions. His exacting mind was able to recall when, after further explanation of a concept or word, he had misunderstood something similar before, and would advise them to replace the word with another.

Ironically, it was his demon priesthood training that enabled Tzan Fu to be a reliable Bible translator. The demon priests learn spiritual terminology which was not used in the common language. Until he left to harvest the fields, Tzan Fu would help the Callaways with Mien language study and translation.

Manc-manc, hnamv hnamv, gorngv gorngv. Slowly slowly, think think, talk talk...

Working on the Bible translations consumed much of the Callaways' time. The book of Mark was mimeographed before Christmas in 1957, and the book of Acts by the next spring. This meant that Tzan Fu was needed more than ever. The spiritual opposition that arose was subtle. There were always jobs to do and people to see for the busy Headman that kept him from being with the Callaways, but eventually the work was done.

After about two years in the village, Lois asked Tzan Fu to tell her again the Mien story of the flood, this time in Mien rather than in Chinese. He said, "Do you really understand more Mien than you do Chinese?" she assured him that she thought so and would like to give it a try. Tzan Fu proceeded.

"This big flood must have happened around the same time as the Noah flood you told us about. Everybody died except one brother and sister. They got into a big gourd. Only the two of them were alive so god asked them to marry, but they hated each other. They traveled far away to find a mate and met a turtle and asked the turtle if there was anyone else left. Turtle said 'no'. They got mad and chopped the turtle up. Then they met the bamboo and asked the bamboo if there was anyone else left. Bamboo said 'no.' They got mad again and chopped the bamboo up. The brother and sister refused to marry and went on either side of a brook. When they each built a fire the smoke went up and came together as it rose up. Then they knew they had to put the turtle together and the bamboo back together. That is why they both look like they are made of little pieces stuck together."

"I understand this, Tzan Fu," Lois exclaimed. "This is a story of the bamboo and the turtle, as well as the flood."

From that time on, Tzan Fu and the other men began to speak to Lois in Mien, and eventually, when the Mien no longer addressed them by their Chinese titles "Teacher Tall" and "Madame Tall," the Callaways felt linguistically accepted. The Mien gave them titles in their own language, "Father Teacher" and "Mother Teacher."

Chapter 10

Bear Attack

Lois will always remember Jiem-Zoih. She saved his life, sewing his face together piece by piece, but she could not save his soul.

He came to their home on a stretcher of blood-soaked shirts twisted over two bamboo poles. That evening had started out peacefully. Lois was putting away the dishes from a supper of rice, green vegetables, and a little homemade sausage mixed in. David was playing quietly on the floor. She started moving toward his little hunched form when she thought she saw something scurry across the floor between his hands, but then there was distant yelling and she glanced away, went to the doorway just as a shirtless young man was pumping his thin arms and running breathlessly up the steep trail to their home. "Bear attack! Bear attack! Mother Teacher! Please help!"

Jiem Zoih was a relative of Tzan Fu. A group of men were hunting deer and had encircled an area, unknowingly trapping a mother bear and her cubs. The bear charged straight for Jiem Zoih. He fumbled to load his old muzzle-loading gun, took aim, but it misfired. The bear pinned him to the ground, took his slight form and wedged it between both paws and bit straight into his face.

"Where is he now?" Lois asked.

"The others are bringing him up on a stretcher. Please Mother

Teacher, he must stay with you. It would be a bad omen if he died in a Mien home."

Lois nodded. C.W. started down the trail to meet them. Lois felt a sickly dread crawl up her throat. She hurriedly had little David go upstairs to his room. A black shiny beetle scurried away from their midst, but Lois didn't notice. She had anticipated a lot of blood everywhere, but it was worse than she had imagined. The bear had bitten into Jiem Zoih at the right temple and bridge of his nose and then twisted, ripping off most of the center of his face. His back was hideously torn by the claws.

With ordinary sewing needles and thread, Lois and C.W. attempted to sew as much of the flesh back onto his face as possible, alternately stitching and treating for shock. Through several trembling hours, most of his face was sewn back together except the bridge of the nose where profuse bleeding began every time they tried to insert the needle. At one point they had to stop completely because of the gushing blood. It was only through the mercy of God that the bleeding stopped.

As Lois sewed and wiped and irrigated, a small crowd of men gathered behind her. There was heated discussion that night about conducting a devil worship ceremony. Such an accident was always caused by the wrath of the spirits. Since the Callaways were nursing him in their home, they decided to take a firm stand on the issue.

"If you choose to have a demon worship ceremony for him, we will not touch him," C.W. said. The ultimatum was difficult, but any time they had to give one, God had never once allowed the result to cast dishonor on His name. Lois knew that this time would be no different.

Throughout the night, prayers were lifted up in the name of Jesus for this man. Even Tzan Fu, as he meticulously took on the tedious job of threading needles, lifted his voice in prayer to God for help. "Jesus demon" was the literal translation of whom he called out to. The prayer itself sounded like a demon chant, but it was Tzan Fu's utmost, and who can say that God did not honor that prayer of the heart?

As the night wore on, they continued stitching. Several times they had to stop to allow Jiem Zoih to rest and treat him for shock.

He needed several pints of blood but the best they could do was to deluge his broken body with sedatives, antibiotics and prayer. During the times of rest, they were given the opportunity to talk with Tzan Fu about God. If nothing else was gained, Lois knew that this was a genuine and precious time of sharing that may not have occurred otherwise.

For the next six weeks, five to six hours a day were dedicated to nursing this man to health. The missionaries gave Jiem Zoih regular injections of penicillin, food, and care. Granny Bet insisted that his wife stay with him. It was only right. Begrudgingly, she did, and helped to nurse him back to health. They prayed for healing. God showed the villagers that no demon worship was necessary. Jiem Zoih lived. Eventually however, despite their best efforts, his nose fell completely off his face, leaving a gaping hole. Only half of his upper lip remained which gave him a bizarre sneering smile fixed on his face. His frightening appearance was too much for his wife to stand. She quietly sought comfort in the arms of another man.

As Jiem Zoih regained his strength, C.W. and Lois would often sit and chat with him. "Jiem Zoih, we have been living here, teaching the Mien for nearly four years. Everyone seems so friendly to us, and sometimes even interested in the Gospel. Why is it," C.W. asked, "that still none of you have taken an open stand for Christ?"

After some thought, Jiem Zoih replied through his torn and swollen lips, "The Mien are afraid of you. I was afraid of you, and would never have come to sleep in your house if I hadn't been so near dead I couldn't help myself. We have been told that when you have converted a number of us you will take us to America to feed us to the giant spirits. We are afraid that you will give us medicine to charm us and we will be converted against our wills."

Although it was encouraging to hear such honesty from Jiem Zoih, it was at the same time, a hard realization that Lois' eyes still appeared "yellow" to the Mien; still the giant white demons.

After many weeks, Jiem Zoih was able to care for himself and cook his own food. The village was impressed with the healing powers of the God of the white foreigner, but they whispered about this man's terrifying appearance. He looked like a demon himself. His wife finally left her disfigured husband for the other man.

One day Lois heard voices calling her as she prepared to make rolls and a loaf of bread. She brushed off her flour-covered hands and ran toward the voices. "Mother Teacher! Father Teacher! Come quickly!"

It had to do with Jiem Zoih again, but this time, he was not the one lying helpless and bleeding. It was his wife. Jiem Zoih had run into Tzan Fu's house in full daylight with a well-sharpened knife, plunged it four times into his wife's chest and then had fled into the jungle. Lois kneeled beside Jiem Zoih's wife. C.W. was already there. The bleeding from the stab wounds was profuse. Lois felt the blood wet her knees as it soaked through her skirt. The flour still between her fingers turned pink. The woman died within minutes of their arrival.

Jiem Zoih was never found. Without his injections, his weakened body would have easily succumbed to infection. M'Lou said that he had enough opium with him to kill himself. If he was dead, his body was probably dragged off by wild animals, but no one knew for sure.

For weeks, the villagers feared that Jiem Zoih, crazed with anger and pain would return to Tzanfuville on a killing spree. Lois cried a little and prayed constantly during those long nights. Nightmares came to little five-year-old David, and so Lois wrote...

> Be quiet in the darkness, Child.
> There's fear enough without
> You telling how you feel at night
> With shadows all about.
> Just wait a while for sunshine, Child.
> And when He gives you peace,
> Then tell about the radiant joy
> That comes when troubles cease.

Peace did eventually come, and troubles ceased if only for a while. The process of the rationalizations: the "what ifs" the "whys" kept Lois awake at night.

Chapter 11

Demons in the Attic

T so ta gwei. "Do big demons." Do a big demon worship. Rules to follow, appeasements to be made, but like the true meaning of Christmas, the rituals and activities sometimes superseded the spirit behind it. It seemed that way to Lois anyway. Even though this was a time of celebration for her Mien friends, a break from the normal sedentary village life, Lois recognized the dark nature of the ceremonies. When Lois first saw Saeng Meng don the black robe and hood of the demon priest, his deeply lined scowl looked even more ominous.

Big sheets of heavy grass paper were cut into pieces about three inches by six inches. A man picked up a metal stamp and struck the paper over and over in a rhythmic fashion. He was making "money" to fool the demons. To imprint the total surface of hundreds of sheets, another man joined the first, and they worked steadily on this task for two days, squatting on the ground beside each other. Two other men were busy writing posters or booklets in big Chinese characters for the occasion. Tzan Fu's father, who always seemed to be doing something related to spirit worship, worked at fastening animal skins onto frames to use as drums.

Pigs and chickens were sacrificed. Spirit doctors mumbled incantations and danced before the spirits. It was an exciting time in the village, with plenty of good food to eat, firecrackers being shot off and children from neighboring villages running together about the hillsides.

After falling into a deep sleep that night, Lois was startled awake at 2:30 AM to movement around Tzan Fu's house next door. Then the rasping blast from the water buffalo horn jolted everyone fully awake. The horn, drum, and cymbals began to work together in a strange, eerie tune. Every few minutes until daybreak, the music would burst forth again, but it was always the same haunting melody.

Centuries of tribal tradition dictated the somber performance of rites for the adults. A small bamboo mat hung before the door indicated that devil worship was in progress. The men of the tribe bowed down before the household spirit shelf and rehearsed a long singsong chant. They believed that this ritual held off the wrath of the spirits and thus warded off sickness or damage to their crops.

As deeply ingrained as this tradition was, Lois was aware of some discontent in the village. Some villagers admitted that demon worship was costly to them, and brought little benefit. With a little coaxing, Lois thought, they might be freed from the tyranny of the ancient customs. Some villagers seriously pondered the alternative of a free life in Christ, but the fear of the demons always proved greater in the end, and tradition usually triumphed. Never having experienced the fear that was a daily part of the demon worshiper's life, it was difficult for Lois to see how threatening her talk of stopping demon worship was to them. It was a safety net. Stopping demon worship made as much sense to the Mien, as standing blindfolded in the middle of the street to a New Yorker. The mystery of where the white people came from, and their "yellow" eyes certainly didn't help their cause. Naturally, rumors abounded. There was one particularly vicious rumor which said that the Westerners wanted the Mien to become Christians so that they could cut their hearts out. Their hearts would then be sent to America to be used to make atomic bombs.

Mien historical chants might have fed into the idea that Lois and C.W. were the descendants of their former cannibal neighbors in China. In these chants, the Mien tell a story of cannibals that were driven away in battle and fled to the east in boats. Innocently enough, when Lois first arrived in the village, she told them that they had come over the ocean from the direction where the sun rises, in boats that flew in the sky. They definitely looked physically big enough to eat some of them whole. So the logical conclusion was that Lois and C.W. needed the lives of Mien Christians to avenge for the lives lost in the ancient battle. Once killed, the hearts would be sent to America in order to feed the giant cannibal spirits, or to make atomic bombs, whichever version was preferred.

It was likely that the opium dealers helped circulate such stories about the westerners because they wanted to keep the Mien from becoming Christians. When a Mien became a Christian, he was encouraged to leave the illegal opium growing business and trust God for his future. This was an enormous leap of faith for the Mien. Opium was in great demand and a sure source of income.

Saeng Meng came to Lois on the Chinese New Year. It had rained all day and he looked concerned.

"This has never happened before," he said, "I am very afraid that there will be a great flood."

Saeng Meng's concern over a great flood proved to be an excellent segue for Lois to talk again about God's faithfulness. After the story of Noah, she assured him that there would be no such flood ever again. He seemed unimpressed and preoccupied with the preparations of further festivities. His response was typical. Lois felt a deep frustration. The life-giving words of Scripture were repeatedly dismissed as light entertainment and diversion from the mundane. If there were other matters to attend to, her words fell like fine bamboo dust on their ears.

After the New Year's celebration, there commenced a series of atonement days. To appease the tiger spirit and the hatchet spirit, Tzanfuville bustled with preparation. Literally translated, "hold the tiger days" and "hold the hatchet day," each ceremony had strict rules. No rice was to be pounded out of the husk, no grass was to be cut for horses, no banana stalks were to be cut for the pigs, no vegetables or other food were to be cut for the people. Cooking and eating were allowed but the use of knives and hatchets was particularly banned lest the hatchet demon be angered.

For the two "tiger days" the trails approaching each Mien

village were blocked with tree branches and no one was allowed to enter or leave the village until the redemption time was up for the tiger demon. Loud noise was taboo. It was odd to see certain women, usually so explosive, trying to be a bit quieter and even chiding their children for shouting.

Saeng Meng put on his stern lecturing face with Lois and said, "There was a Chinese merchant's mule that was killed by a tiger below our village six months ago." Saeng Meng grew smug, "It was because he had not kept tiger day."

During this time, there were many more Mien visitors to the cabin than usual. They loved looking through the Viewmaster, listening to the Mien gospel records, and looking over the posters and filmstrips. It was a wonderful opportunity for language study and witness.

The following month the village was barricaded again to make peace with the wind demon. Later Lois noted in her journal, "snake day" and "fire day," and how many others she lost track of, she did not know.

Even the Cabin in the Clouds was suspected of evil. "The foreigners have demons in their attic." To the Mien, the attic was a secret, hidden place where they had never been invited to go. It was suspect of all sorts of evil. It was time to start dispelling the rumors. The benign little attic, Lois' only place of escape from the constant observation and scrutiny of the village, had to be exposed.

The attic was primarily used to dry clothes. Laundry for a family of seven was hung to dry while the house stood in a continuous cloud for three monsoon months. It also made a convenient place to store staple groceries since the best store for western foodstuffs was in Bangkok, 500 miles away, at least five or six days travel from the mountain cabin. Sleeping bags were hung in the attic by wires from the ceiling to discourage the rats from making their nests there.

At one end of the attic was a little nook. Lois' early morning studies were done there. Most days she could look out of the window down on the clouds that hid the Mekong River and at the lovely evergreen clothed mountain peaks pushing up to the hazy sky above. One of her greatest joys was to greet the day there, looking to the hills, and to seek God the Father from whom flowed all help for every hardship. It was her place of respite, often joined by small David at five a.m. for daily talks with each other and with God.

Now her refuge was about to be invaded. Privacy was interpreted as secrecy. Secrecy was only necessary if there were dark evils to be hidden. There was no other place where any well-kept secrets might be hidden. Every other inch of the house had been inspected by frequent visitors. "What is that?" they would ask as they peered over Lelan and Mark's shoulders as they ate their sausage and bread. "Why do you scrub your kitchen floor?" Sometimes Lois wondered too with all the people and an occasional pig wandering in and out all day. Still, there was that part of being Lois that felt proud even for a brief moment of cleanliness.

A day was set to dispel the rumors. On "attic day" Lois fried mounds of doughnuts, which she hoped the Mien would like since they were less sweet than cookies or cake, and made gallons of Kool-Aid. Then C.W. invited them over to see everything in the attic—a holiday to see the neighbors' secrets.

The people of the village gathered on the badminton court in front of the clinic door. No one was willing to venture inside the house. Lois served Kool-Aid and doughnuts outside as they visited with the people and listened in on their comments on the refreshments. The Kool-Aid met with immediate disapproval—too sweet. The doughnuts were sampled out of curiosity and declared very inferior to sticky rice cakes mixed with charred straw. The great crowd milled around on the badminton court. No one was even brave enough to venture up to the second story, much less the attic.

Finally, Lois held out her hand to Granny Bet. "Come on Granny, go up with me." She looked about hesitantly and said, "If someone will go with me, I'll go."

Reluctantly, Granny May half whispered, "I'll go with you, I guess." She took Granny Bet's hand and Granny Bet reached for Lois' extended hand. Lois felt Granny's hand tremble. It was just then that Lois realized the tangible fear that gripped the village. Dear, spunky Granny Bet was not just nervous, she was deathly afraid.

Lois kept her tone light as they went up the first flight of stairs. They looked at the bookcase wall. A demon priest in the village might have one or two books in his house, both for doing demon worship. Granny Bet said, "Whatever do you do with so many books?" Lois didn't know if Granny believed her when she said that they enjoyed reading stories and learning.

As Lois led them to the bedroom, they touched the spring and cotton mattresses. They marveled that anyone could sleep comfortably on a bed so soft. A bamboo floor with a horsehair blanket on it was firmer and better.

They looked at the pantry filled with cans of peas, corn, baby food, and oatmeal. Granny Bet looked long and hard at the oatmeal with the picture of the Quaker man on the front, and the smiling baby on a jar of strained green beans. She looked at Granny May and then at Lois with a confused and frightened look. Lois realized what was happening...canned peas had a picture of peas, canned corn had a picture of corn, and now canned man? Baby flesh? She quickly explained that sometimes the picture says who will eat the food, not what is inside the can. There was some visible relief in their eyes. The cannibal issue deflated a bit, and Lois continued with her tour.

Meanwhile some of the Mien boys had also ventured up to the attic with second son, Mark, scrutinizing everything and speculating its purpose.

"Hey, that's where you keep your demons," one of the boys was pointing to the sleeping bags which were hanging from the attic rafters.

Mark took his bag down, spread it out, crawled in, zipped it up and pantomimed sleeping. Lois said that they were only used on trips and that they were stored up high so that the rats wouldn't make a nest in them.

The custom of the Mien was to gather the bones of the deceased grandparents after cremation, bundle the bones in red cloth or plastic and dangle it from the rafters of their houses until the demon priests declared the auspicious day for burial. Sometimes the bones were carried to a new place when the family moved and the bones were buried there. It must have appeared to the Mien that the

Callaways had several generations of bones waiting to be laid to rest. If they were indeed the cannibal ancestors, they would especially want to return to their ancestral land to be "gathered to their fathers." Lois kept mental note of the rumors being shot down.

The two grannies and Mark's friends had descended to the first floor unharmed to a wide-eyed and curious reception. A large group followed Lois for the next tour, and this continued for the rest of the exhausting day. Several times, Lois was asked about the sleeping bags.

"It is only our place to rest," she would reply, and that was all Lois really wanted for her Mien friends. To rest.

Chapter 12

Faith Stories

I n July of 1959, two American soldiers were killed while watching a movie just outside of Bienhoa, the headquarters of a South Vietnamese army division. When the lights switched on for the reels to be changed, guerrillas sprayed the room with bullets, killing Major Buis and Master Sergeant Ovnand, two South Vietnamese guards, and an eight-year-old Vietnamese boy. A small article in Time magazine reported this insidious event. Some saw it as the inception of the Vietnam Era, the euphemism given for the war that was never formally declared.[4]

Lois with Mary Baldock and Mien on
mountain trail (1958)

In September of that same year, the Callaways moved back to the hills of Thailand.

Despite the harbinger of military restlessness casting ominous shadows over Asia, Lois trekked up the hill back to her Cabin in the Clouds. She was met with the news that Granny Bet was ill. Lois was at her side as soon as the buckets and boxes of supplies were set safely inside her home.

Granny Bet

Lois entered the dark smoky house, using the customary greeting, "Biauv-ziouv yiem fai?" "Is the master of the house home?". Granny Bet's small frame was still and hardly distinguishable from the irregular shadows of the room. Lois glanced over at the altar. There were no offerings there. She whispered a prayer against the evil spirits, and a prayer of thanks for God's provision. She also prayed for good words for her dear Granny Bet. Lois knelt next to her and a thin arm rose up to hold her hand. Granny Bet was succumbing slowly to the degenerative effects of cardiac beriberi.

"I thought you were not coming back."

"You are my friend, Granny Bet, and I will do everything I can to help you."

"My friend, Mwang Meng, has told me that I should become a Christian before I die."

Lois knew that Mwang Meng had been a Christian for about five years. She smiled at the toothless wrinkled face before her. How hard it must have been for her, the grand matriarch of the village to take orders from another, even if they were given in love.

"I wanted to believe for a long time but my husband and son would not give their permission. I told this to Mwang Meng, and now I tell this to you, Mother Teacher."

Lois had not often heard Granny Bet refer to her as "Mother Teacher."

"You know, Granny Bet, your son, Tzan Fu is softening...just like you have softened."

A toothless smile. A slight grimace. "Then I can become a Christian."

Lois smiled again. Since Tzan Fu's father died two years ago, and Tzan Fu was softening, things seemed hopeful. Lois gave her friend's hand a squeeze, much like on the day Granny bravely went up the stairs to the attic with her. She left with the promise to return soon.

Later that afternoon, as Lois was unpacking cereal, books, and Kool-Aid, Tzan Fu dropped by to talk with C.W. He had an upright and official look about him as he announced to the missionaries that his mother wanted to become a Christian, but first he needed to ascertain the various beliefs and practices of this foreign religion.

"What do I have to do as a Christian?"

"You must believe that Jesus died for your sins and turn away from your old life of worshiping demons and trust Jesus."

"Do I need to sacrifice to Jesus?"

"No, he sacrificed His life for you."

Tzan Fu had heard the story many times in mini Easter pageants and on the flannel graph stories, and yet there was a persistent look of puzzlement. Maybe it was fear.

"Did your father buy your wife for you?" Tzan Fu asked C.W.

"No, she roped me into it." C.W. laughed. Tzan Fu waited for the translation.

"Don't confuse him, Dub," she smiled. "Tzan Fu, we choose each other in love when we marry." The questioning went on for a good hour or so.

"How do Christians marry?"

"What do you do at a funeral if you don't have demon worship?"

The next morning Tzan Fu came to call on the Callaways again. "Mother Teacher, my mother wants you to come over. She wants to enter Christ," Tzan Fu added, "I myself intend to become a Christian some day, so I see no reason why my mother should not accept the Lord now if she wants to."

When Lois went into the house, she found Granny desperately ill and fearful of death. Granny Bet had broken off demon worship and opium addiction before her illness as a first step, now she readied herself for the final step into eternity. She confessed her faith in Christ and turned from the spirits. Lois could only pray for her healing and give such medication as was indicated. Through the mercy of the Lord, her weak heart was kept beating. For two weeks the Callaways battled with prayer and medical injections for her life. She became very thin and weak after that ordeal. Her faith remained steadfast, and at times Lois sensed that Granny had been put forth as a tester for the family. Most of them said, "We will slowly, slowly watch to see if Granny gets well. If she does, then we too, will believe."

"The Matriarch," that once sharp-tongued, selfish, self-seeking woman, had accepted Jesus into her heart. Granny Bet had softened and changed. Loving her through her selfish demands and manipulations seemed easy in retrospect. It was about establishing trust all along. It was worth it. "The Matriarch" now reigned with grace. She was the first in Tzanfuville to make a stand for Christ.

The daily walks to her house to care for her diseased body, the daily prayers for her and with her, were quietly watched by the village. Weakened by the beriberi and quite senile, she seemed slow to comprehend the teaching. Yet others sat along side listening as the Callaways taught, and she in her faith declared that she wanted to be a "Jesus person."

In 1960, while the Callaways were in India enrolling the children in school, a letter arrived for them from a fellow-missionary, Mel Byers. Granny Bet had died. He wrote:

"I have just...performed my first Mien funeral. I have never felt more welcome in their midst. They talked at some length about the whole village coming into Christ. One man, once convinced that he didn't have to make any paper money to propitiate the demons for this funeral, seemed quite pleased and said 'I guess it is true, the whole village doesn't have to go in at once, a person can be a Christian by himself.'"

When Granny Bet died, Tzan Fu and the villagers generally agreed that she would have wanted a Christian funeral, and she should have one. The poisonous grip that the demons had on their lives grew impotent with each stand they took. As they did not insist upon the usual demon rites Mel was free to conduct a service of hope. There were a few of the women who were concerned that if the rites were not performed, Granny's spirit would return to harass them, but the Christian funeral proceeded nonetheless. When Mel Byers arrived in the village, he found an overwhelming spirit of helpfulness and cordiality. Not only did the Mien tribespeople seek his advice concerning every detail of the funeral, that it be done in the way Jesus would have them do, but also they listened well to the witness which Mel gave. His words now had meaning, for they had seen one of their own live and die for Him.

Tzan Fu

Headman Tzan Fu (right)
with his father (1958)

When Tzan Fu was twenty-nine years old, he took a social smoke of opium and became addicted. He was one of the men who decided to "take the cure" for seven days at the bamboo house. He asked if he could be cured of worshiping the evil spirits. Lois assured him that they knew One who could deliver him from that curse, and warned him that unless he accepted that One as his personal Lord, he would not have real victory over the spirits or opium. Tzan Fu was free of opium for about three months. His second wife was an opium addict and soon he was back to three pipes a day. Through his failing, Lois learned a valuable spiritual lesson. Physically Tzan Fu was cured, but emotionally and spiritually he was not. He needed God's help to remain free.

One day, some fellow missionaries were visiting the Callaways. Lois made bread slathered with homemade peanut butter, and hot tea. The morning had been set aside for prayer. They met upstairs, when half way through the prayer time, Tzan Fu headed up the stairs, unannounced.

Introductions were made, as the missionaries were new to the village. One guest greeted Tzan Fu and said, "It is good to meet you. We were just praying for you."

Tzan Fu left abruptly. For many days Lois did not see him. When C.W. visited him at his home, he seemed uneasy and wary. It was a long time until Tzan Fu was able to rest easily again, for he thought that the prayers made on his behalf were those of black magic. A priest was often paid to make prayers and incantations for relatives, but "to pray" for someone who was not a family member could only mean a curse.

On the nights when the Mien gathered about the fire, conversations about opium, horses and hogs generally prevailed. On one such night, there was a lull in the conversation, and Tzan Fu directed a question at Nai Brong, a Thai porter and a new Christian.

"Nai Brong, have you entered Christ?"

"Yes, I have entered Christ. I was a sinner. My heart was full of sin." Tzan Fu's expression remained impassive. He did not understand the Thai word for "sin."

Nai Brong continued, "When I say that my heart was full of sin, that means that my heart was filthy. But Jesus washed it clean with His blood. He died for me and by dying he washed my heart clean. There's nothing in this world—nothing—that can wash our hearts clean but the blood of Jesus."

Tzan Fu would listen carefully to testimonies like Nai Brong's and to the Bible teachings. Lois often wondered if his father had anything to do with Tzan Fu's resistance to conversion. His father was an old wrinkled fixture of a man always seated on the far side of the fire, always with the smoke obscuring his view. He had long been the demon priest for his village. By rights this son, Tzan Fu, would also be understudy for the demon priesthood. Tzan Fu could not turn to Christ without much opposition from his father.

Many Mien told the Callaways that when others believe they would too. Tzan Fu assured them that when he "entered Christ" nearly all of this village would too.

During another of the many taped messages from Brother Six, the villagers gathered around to hear the words from the "word gathering box."

"Tzan Fu, if you believe all your people will believe. If you do not believe they will be afraid to and you will be keeping them from coming to Christ."

Tzan Fu and several villagers stood quietly for a moment. Then one woman said, "Tzan Fu, do you believe or don't you?"

"Of course I believe!" replied Tzan Fu. Then Lois knew that he had at some point responded in his heart, but he could not make the break from the opium lifestyle. He was again addicted, and the monetary gain from his opium fields was far too lucrative to give up. She noticed that Tzan Fu started a few coffee trees. He appeared to be considering an alternative source of income.

Tzan Fu would often draw near to the Lord and then suddenly pull away. Lois noticed this pattern in her relationships with the village people. Withdrawal. Even when there seemed to be a glimmer of hope and understanding, withdrawal always followed. Regular visitors started to avoid the Callaways. Interest turned to apathy or fear.

It was through Brother Six that the Callaways became firmly entrenched in the Mien mainstream. He was the first Mien man that the Callaways knew of who had become a Christian. Brother Six was the headman of a village so he commanded respect. He had warned Lois once that because of the fear of black magic, she should not try to persuade anyone outside her own clan to believe. Not belonging to any clan, the missionaries did not know what to do. During their next visit to his village, Brother Six stepped forward to fulfill this need. He adopted Lois into his own Bienh or Phan clan, making her the younger sister of his wife. C.W. was adopted into the Leiz or Lee clan. He gave C.W. the Mien name Tzan Hiaang Lee as though he was a brother to Tzan Fu.

"Most of the people in your village are either Leiz or Bienh clan people. This way one or the other of you will be able to witness to nearly everyone in your village." This was one more tentative thread of trust to pull the Callaways closer to the Mien. Still, they had to prove their harmlessness before the Mien would even consider accepting their love, their faith, their God.

When Tzan Fu married a second wife, who was staunchly opposed to the Gospel, he remained somewhat distant. However when he developed cancer behind the eyes, he occasionally sought out the missionaries for medical advice. Around the same time, his first wife developed abdominal cancer. When Tzan Fu and his first wife died on the same day, there were whisperings that her spirit had caused his death because he took a second wife. He never firmly took a verbal stand for Christ.

Granny May

Granny Mae (1958)

Another red muffled Granny close to Lois' heart was Granny May. Granny May was a widow. One day in June she came to the Cabin in the Clouds with a small gift of vegetables. Abruptly she announced that she would come the next day and believe in Jesus. C.W. explained to her that if she were to follow Jesus she should cut off all devil worship and sin and fully surrender to Jesus.

"I must plant opium one more time. Next year I will sell all my opium and will be baptized. Right now I want to break demon worship and begin to worship Jesus."

Lois pointed to the thin charm strings tied about her wrist to ward off evil spirits. "Granny, let's destroy all of your old devil things."

Granny May decisively held out her delicate little wrist to the missionaries and said, "Will you cut them off now?"

C.W. said, "I'll be glad to, but first let us pray." So in simple Mien, C.W. gave thanks to God for this great step of faith. Hidden behind those thin dirty strings were generations of strong bondage to superstition. This was no small act for this brave little woman. Since she was a child, Granny May had seen the prominent demon shelf in the center of her home. Daily conversations dealt at length with the evil spirits. The spirits had to be taken into consideration at every turn of the trail, at every drop of the hoe, or at every chop with the axe.

Granny May had often expressed her wish to be free from the spirits but admitted to still being afraid of them. Some months earlier, she had asked, "What will become of us if we believe in Jesus and you leave to go back to America? Will the demons then come back to harm us and will we then have no means to appease them?"

Lois explained that her trust must be in Christ, not people.

So now she had made her decision. There was her outstretched arm and she waited for C.W. to cut the strings. He did, and threw them into the little wood stove.

"Tomorrow," she said, "I'm going to bring over my demon worship things for you to burn," then thinking a moment she said, "Or would it be all right for me to bring them now?"

"That would be fine."

Granny May returned with a shoulder bag containing imitation paper money, a few sticks, a small iron, and small cups used for offering wine to the spirits. As she broke the cups and C.W. buried the iron, she offered a spontaneous plea on her own to Jesus, and twice later asked C.W. to pray on her behalf. With an audible sigh of relief, she went home.

Chapter 13

Paul Shen

T he radio was crackling with news that there was war in Laos. Communist messages in Chinese urged tribal people, especially the Hmong, to join with the communist forces to "gain their freedom from Laos." The static voices never mentioned that "freedom" meant life under communist rule.

Some found that accepting the new Chinese ruler, Mao Tse Dong was made smoother by an interesting coincidence. The Hmong tribespeople were called Miao or Meo in the Chinese language. This sounded very close to Mao. A popular thought was that destiny had brought Mao Tse Dong as a fulfillment of Hmong prophecy to liberate the Hmong people. Those who resisted often sided with the American forces.

Despite the violent political upheaval in nearby Laos, life in Thailand continued as usual for the Callaways in their little Mien village, except for a slow filtering in of Chinese Nationalist soldiers of Chiang Kai Shek's army. These men married Mien girls, and melted into the milieu. The Chinese were trading their western style clothing for Mien homespun jackets to conceal their identity as illegal immigrants. Lois often joked that the only way to tell if a man was Chinese was if he wore Mien clothing.

The Thai government seemingly chose to close its eyes to the immigrant situation, knowing that the Chinese Nationalists were a good cushion against the communist infiltration into the Lao-Thai border. The Thai government, in fact, had a tacit agreement with a Chinese general, requiring him to maintain law and order among his troops in exchange for unchallenged residence in border areas. Some of these soldiers would stop by and visit the Callaways, and eventually C.W. and Lois befriended many of them. Often, when at leisure, they came to sit in their home, put on records, and read books. In the crowded clinic bookcases, the Callaways made room for Chinese Bibles, Christian books and tracts. They even added a number of Chinese preaching and hymn records to the Mien collection. C.W. and Lois had the opportunity to share the gospel with them, and also to expand their Chinese vocabulary. They often sat and listened to them talk among themselves, making language notes to themselves. It was a relaxed and congenial atmosphere.

CW baptizing Mien Believers (1970)

There were Christians among these troops who were hungry for teaching and fellowship, and even a few new converts, like Paul Shen who had been baptized by C.W. in a cold mountain stream. Paul was special to the Callaways: intelligent and honest with an uplifting freshness in his newly found faith. Lois liked him very much.

Early one morning, the former headman, Saeng Meng came to the house and asked C.W. to go with him down the trail a bit. He had something to show him. C.W. followed, curious. Saeng Meng led him to the murdered body of a Chinese man lying face up on the trail. C.W. recognized this man at once: Lao Lee: Saeng Meng's son-in-law. He was a polite and quiet fellow, and had been in the home many times to chat. This man had married one of Saeng Meng's daughters for a sizable bride price. It was rumored that even though his daughter had plans to marry another man, the cost of maintaining Saeng Meng's opium habit made it impossible for him to refuse the generous bride price offered by the Chinese fellow.

"Who could have done such a thing?" C.W. asked.

"I don't know," Saeng Meng replied, "I heard Laotian voices last night around my son-in-law's house and thought it was some kind of business deal. Then I heard gunshots."

There was talk that Lao Lee had been involved in robberies across the border in Laos. It was assumed that the Lao had come to get revenge.

"Everyone was afraid to go out until dawn," Saeng Meng continued. "When morning came I walked here and found him like this. Then I walked to your house. I felt you should know all the facts in case anyone came around asking questions."

A messenger was sent on the two-day walk to the county seat to ask the police to come and investigate the murder. Meanwhile, there was nothing to do but leave the decomposing body there by the trail until the police arrived for questioning.

The events of that day made the villagers nervous. When Lois stepped outside next day, she saw that the village was full of movement. Many of the villagers were laden with bedrolls, cooking pots and bulging shoulder bags, heading down the trail. It was too late for the corn and rice harvest, and too early for the opium harvest, and much too cold and windy for so much activity. This was an exodus. It was time to hide.

Two days later, the clinic was swarming with people needing malaria and cough medicine, and lots of aspirin for every imaginable pain. Lois looked up from counting pills to see M'Lou walking toward her, pushing her way to the front.

She said, "Big Sister, come with us and hide in the jungles. The Chinese have sent a letter with a bullet in it, threatening to shoot every Mien man, woman, or child on sight. We are afraid. They are about to attack the village to get revenge for Lao Lee's death. It's not safe to stay in the village. Come with us to the jungles until the worst of this is over."

"No, I won't go," Lois replied with a matter of fact tone, "but I'll be here if you need me. God will protect us. We will stay here and trust in Him."

Lois remained calm to M'Lou, but inside, her head was spinning. How to protect the children?

"Jeni, let's build a fort...a camping place...someplace special for you to sleep tonight."

"Camping! Where?"

"How about right here under the stairway?" Jeni would be farther from the thin, rickety walls in case gunfire did break out. "See, and we'll stack up the pillows like this and it will make a big soft wall."

"I like this game, Mommy!"

By the time her children were safely tucked away and sleeping, Lois was exhausted and emotionally spent. She crawled into her own bed and fell asleep quickly despite all that churned within her. Her sleep was dark, dreamless and brief. Before the morning rays could awaken her, she was startled awake by the abrupt voices of the Thai District Magistrate and his soldiers in the house. They were in search of any recalcitrant Chinese illegals in the area. On that bitterly cold and wet December day, Lois went through the motions of her work, heeding the constant calls for medicine from the Mien, all the while acutely aware of the shadowy presence of the Thai soldiers moving in and out among the villagers.When the District Magistrate and his soldiers arrived at the scene of the crime, they took one look, and said, "He is very dead! Bury him!" This concluded the murder investigation.

Toward evening, Paul Shen slipped quietly into the house. He asked C.W. and Lois to hide him. He had heard that the Mien would shoot any Chinese on sight and was afraid. Paul's situation was made even more complicated because of his newfound faith.

"Because I am a Christian, I have told the Chinese that I will not join them in the massacre they are planning to avenge Lao Lee. So now the Chinese too, are my enemies."

"You must stay with us, Paul," Lois said, and ushered him into C.W.'s study. They improvised a bed on C.W.'s large desk and assured him that he would be safe there.

"We will hand you food from the inside entrance. You'll have to slip out to the bathroom on the back porch. Otherwise stay quietly in the room."

This seemed to be a fine plan, until they remembered the presence of the District Magistrate in the area. He was there to arrest illegal Chinese immigrants. Paul was still technically an illegal alien. Since the murder, the agreement between the Thai government and the Chinese general had weakened. The general had failed to keep law and order among his men in the area, and the Thai law responded by taking a more vigilant and aggressive posture in the surrounding villages. Paul's status was precarious.

If C.W. and Lois were caught harboring a refugee from the law, then they stood the chance of losing their visas. That night, C.W. talked quietly with Paul, explaining the dilemma. "Paul," he said, "I feel I have no choice but to tell the District Magistrate you are here. I will ask for mercy from him for you since you, as a Christian, are simply trying to stay out of harm's way. We will pray that he will 'forget' that I told him you were here."

Paul agreed. "As a Christian," he replied, "I have to be honest. Do what you have to do, Father Teacher, God will take care of me. I know that."

It was early morning when the Thai soldiers started their search of the area for any Chinese that might be hiding. They found none. The Chinese men had been given plenty of advanced warning and were hiding in the jungle. Their Mien wives took food to them each night. Lois often saw their shadowy figures moving about in the darkness.

C.W. sought out the Magistrate that day. They became acquainted, and he promptly invited him and his bodyguard to their home for dinner that evening. Perhaps a full stomach would allow for a greater understanding of their situation, and compassion for their friend Paul.

During the meal, C.W. was able to tell the Magistrate about Paul and ask for leniency for him. The Magistrate answered only with a thoughtful, "Hmmm," and resumed conversation about other matters. Lois quietly ate, elated that he did not pursue the issue further. She silently thanked God as it seemed clear that the Magistrate had chosen to close his eyes to Paul's presence.

The Magistrate briefly questioned C.W. about the murder. He replied honestly that he knew nothing, save for what the Mien had already told him. The subject was dropped and the conversation moved on to other pleasantries. Paul would be safe after all.

Four days later, the District Magistrate and his men found themselves ready to leave with no captive Chinese in tow. Empty hands might signify a failed mission. He came to the home.

"Where is the young man, Paul? The law you know... I have to take him."

They were crushed. Paul, however, was in good spirits as he left. He carried only a small tribal shoulder bag, and had only the clothes that he wore. He had no coat, nothing to keep him warm from the wet December winds.

It was with much sadness that Lois dispensed medicine the next day. She kept seeing the image of Paul's slight frame walking away from the village, his compact bag bouncing against his body, surrounded by the well-armed soldiers of the Magistrate.

Not long after Paul was arrested, C.W. had to go to Chiang Mai to bring the older children home from boarding school. Lois missed him and the children terribly. Paul's arrest had made a deep sorrowful wound in her heart, and the drizzle of loneliness added to her pain. She found some comfort in the thought that they would all be together again soon. But today she was alone.

A hard and lonely day at the clinic was made less so by the chattering presence of her Mien friends. As Lois gave Granny Goy her small, folded packet of medicine, she turned to leave. Then turning back, she leaned over to pat Lois' arm and pulled on her sleeve so that she might speak directly into her ear. She whispered, "I just wish Saeng Meng hadn't done this. Just look at all the trouble he's gotten all of us into."

"What do you mean, Granny?" but Lois knew from her eyes what she was saying. Saeng Meng, the former headman, had killed his own son-in-law. Saeng Meng unflinchingly lied about finding Lao Lee's body at the side of the trail. Lois wanted to hear more. Slowly, slowly, the details of the truth were revealed.

Before his own murder, Lao Lee had boasted that when the opium harvest was over, he would methodically murder his father-in-law, Saeng Meng, then Tzan Fu, who was the Big Chief, and other headmen in neighboring villages. Saeng Meng had met his challenge in customary tribal form. He planned to strike first. Two days later, Lao Lee was dead.

As Lois went to bed that night, she pushed back the shutters just enough to peek out at the village above her. She had been told that the Chinese had a large cache of guns and ammunition at the foot of the mountain. The trail up the mountain ran between the badminton court and the Headman's house. The rest of the village was above, and she could see the younger village men patrolling, with their guns, on the ledge above the house.

If it was true that the Chinese were poised below, waiting for the departure of the District Magistrate and his soldiers, then the battle could be as soon as tomorrow. The battlefield would be the badminton court. Lois was tired. Knowing that tomorrow would be another day at the clinic with the sick, she prayed that there would be no casualties from the battle to join them. "Lord, You never slumber nor sleep. Please keep watch while I sleep, and prepare me for tomorrow." He did.

The next morning there was no gunfire, and there was a peaceful stillness in the cool air. In the clinic there was a bustling of activity surrounding Lois. After the visit from the Magistrate, the villagers were still cautious and often sent one able-bodied assertive adult to collect medication for the entire clan. There was a great demand for medicines and Lois was busy, but she kept one eye on the badminton court. Then the clamor was over. By noon everyone had returned to the deep jungles. Lois was free to do her letter writing and translating work upstairs.

In the late afternoon, she heard a familiar voice calling to her in Chinese from below. "Madame Tall! It is me! Paul!" Lois rushed downstairs to find Paul Shen, radiant and healthy.

Her mind raced with questions, and she actually blurted out a few, "Did you run away? Are you hungry? Did they hurt you?" Waves of relief and joy swept over Lois and she praised the Lord.

They sat down to a cup of tea. He relished the hot drink. Refreshed, he told Lois his story.

"One evening on the trail, the District Magistrate and his soldiers pitched camp, and then left. They left me unshackled and unsupervised. I was alone. I thought about running away, but where would I go with night so near? And would that be the right thing to do? So I chose to stay where I was. I built a fire. When they arrived back at camp, the soldiers were shocked to find me tending the fire, and waiting for their return. The Magistrate said he was impressed with my integrity. Since I could speak a little Thai, he often used me as an interpreter. He used me to interrogate the Chinese soldiers who were infiltrating all the Thai borders. As a statement of his trust and respect, the Magistrate sent me back home to pack so that I might return home with him to live in Chiang Khong."

Lois smiled broadly. That year, the other Chinese of the village spent most of the chilly winter nights hiding out in the jungle whenever the Thai Border Police made a foray into the area; all the Chinese, save one. Lois was comforted and reassured by the thought of Paul resting easily in the warmth and safety of the District Magistrate's own home. It was integrity's reward. Lois wrote these words as she reflected on all that had transpired in this young believer's life:

> The shadow lingered on his face,
> The puzzled frown.
> The consciousness of sin had come—
> The heart bowed down.
> In deep contrition there he found
> The Love of Christ,
> Who lifts, redeems, transforms and fills
> With joy unpriced.
> He walked with Him the narrow path
> To Calvary
> And rose, transfigured by a love
> That men could see.

Paul would, from time to time, visit his spiritual home up in the mountains. Each time, Lois found him to be the same as ever, fresh, energetic and full of faith, his compact Chinese New Testament peaking out from his shirt pocket. The last time they saw Paul, he had come down from Burma where he had joined the Chinese Nationalist Army in exile. Still with his New Testament, but now with the responsibilities of supporting a wife and small children, they cherished the moments with him. As he turned to leave, Lois recalled his figure walking into the forest surrounded by the armed and frustrated Thai soldiers just a few years earlier. Somehow he seemed taller this time.

Chapter 14

In the Communist Wake

*CW and Lois doing Bible translation
with Fu Tzan (1965)*

*CW and Lois at their home in
Chiangkham (1970)*

Lois teaching Mien (1970)

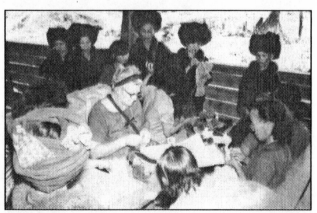

Lois distributing embroidery materials (1974)

The communists were on the move. A Thai official told the Callaways that for their safety, they must soon leave Tzanfuville. The Callaway family hastily packed and, along with all the other villagers, left for the lowlands. The Cabin in the Clouds was rented for a time to a nationalist Chinese man for $15.00 a month before he too, had to flee.

The house itself was then occupied for a while by the communists, but they soon realized that with its three stories and broad roofline it was a clearly visible target from the sky, so they tore it down. They stripped each thoughtfully laid board, and used the rollable aluminum roofing to build temporary lean-to shelters in the jungle. By the early 1960's, Tzanfuville was completely deserted. Eventually the entire village of Tzanfuville was taken apart, and the jungle grew over its remains

Communist propagandists along the Lao/Thai border were actively seeking and recruiting the village people to fight their cause against the Thai government by sowing lies and fostering discontent. The Thai government had had enough. They ordered all the tribes off the mountains east of Chiangkham. "Get out. You have twenty-four hours, then the bombs will begin to fall." It was time to clear out the communists.

In 1970 secret negotiations began between North Vietnam and the United States. The newly elected president, Mr. Richard Nixon, started to pull ground forces from Vietnam soon after his inauguration. The United States seemed to be unable to publicly admit that it was abandoning its ally.[5] The United States was fumbling for closure to the Vietnam War.

Meanwhile, Lois ever vigilant in her ministry to gain insights for Mien literacy books, attended a literacy workshop in South Vietnam. Missionaries there took her to a Mien tribe village. The entire village had moved down from North Vietnam. Upon finding her fluent in Mien, they asked her, "What kind of Mien are you?" (This meant, "From what clan are you?")

Because of Brother Six's earlier insight to make Lois and C.W. a part of their family, Lois was able to reply with confidence, "I am Bien clan, younger sister of Guei Ching's wife."

The elder of the Bien clan in that village was elated. "Oh! You are a member of our family. Come to our house tomorrow and we will prepare a feast for you." Lois went gladly. As they feasted on roasted pork and spiced vegetables, she had the chance to tell them of the story of Jesus who had become the Lord of many of the Bien clan people. They listened and that night, rejoiced together. Mother Teacher's figure towered over the diminutive Mien like a spire of hope in the midst of the screaming terror of war.

When the United States signed the Paris Agreement in January of 1973, it pledged to withdraw all its forces from Vietnam. The Prime Minister of Laos, Prince Souvanna Phouma, feared a similar withdrawal of support from Laos, and pleaded with Henry Kissinger: "The very survival of Laos rests on your shoulders...we must count on our great friends the Americans to help us survive." In just one month's time, however, the Vientiane Agreement was signed. It called for a cease-fire in Laos, a coalition government, and the end of American air support. In June of 1974, the last Air America plane left Laos and the mountain tribal people that were trained and hired by the C.I.A, were left to fend for themselves. Mountain people like Yoon Choy became refugees. They carried what they owned and sought refuge in Thailand.

In 1975, the year the Americans airlifted many out of the clutches of communism and certain death, the Callaways went on furlough to the States. Refugees began to pour out of Laos into Thailand as they fled over the Mekong River. Camps and temporary holding centers were hastily erected. When they returned to Thailand from furlough in 1976, Lois and C.W. lived in Chiangkham but worked with the Mien in the village of Rom Yen which means "Cool Shade." Inherent in that meaning is "pleasant-ness." They called it "Pleasantville," and they started a small Mien church there. Several times a week, they would visit the refugee camps and help ease the barrage of needs while the larger relief organizations took a bit more time to establish themselves. What they had was very little; medicine, bandages and words of comfort, but they stretched everything as far as they could.

Across the Mekong River from Lois, Yoon Choy was still in Laos making plans to escape to Thailand. He was married and his wife, Mae, was his treasure. All he wanted to do was to keep his family together. For most of his life, he had been running from the communists, and Thailand might be a place to rest. He did not tell his wife of his plans for escape. When it came time to sell their corn, Yoon Choy accompanied his wife down the mountain to the edge of the Mekong River. Money in hand, the transaction made, he placed the money into Mae's hands and told her that she must go now to Thailand, and he turned to go back to the village. Go alone? Mae was not prepared. She was frightened and tried to put the money back into her husband's hands.

"I have nothing with me. I cannot go now."

Yoon Choy shoved the money back into her hands.

"You only need the money."

"I am not ready." Her small body shook with each breath.

"There is no better time."

"I have to say good-bye to my parents."

"There will be a reunion on the other side. You only have to find your way to Chiang Khong. My parents will be there." Yoon Choy turned and left Mae standing at the Mekong River alone. Mae looked around the crowd of people. She knew she had to go. Her husband had helped the Americans so he was as good as dead if they stayed in Laos. She needed to find a boat to get to Thailand. Once there, how hard could it be? Drawing strength from her thoughts, Mae pushed through the crowds toward the river's shore.

"Mae!" It was a friend from the village. Her eyes reflected that same fearful emptiness.

"We will travel together. The two tiny women clutched each other and boarded a boat. They paid an exorbitant sum to enter into a new and unknown life.Many entered Thailand by the city of Chiang Saen, where huge empty buildings served as holding centers. Men and women were thrown together and locked in. Rape and robbery were common in the hidden recesses, and this is where Mae found herself after leaving Laos. After one sleepless night, she paid off the Thai guard with some of the money that Yoon Choy had given her from their corn harvest and she made her way to Chiang Saen Refugee Camp. The refugee camps filled up quickly. Waves of people had fled the anti-communist encampments on the Thai border and in Laos and wound up behind barbed wire in a huge clearing, devoid of all greenery.

Mae waited several weeks before Yoon Choy was able to cross the border. When Yoon Choy arrived, Mae had already been swallowed up in the monotony of the camp, and she was sick—morning sickness. Each day was the same. Wake up and get water from the well. Eat what was available, if there was any food at all. Say a kind word to the sick, for they may die tomorrow. Walk for miles it seemed, along piles of human feces to find a place to relieve yourself and go to sleep to awaken to the same nightmare again. Chiang Saen was meant to be a temporary location, so there were no provisions or facilities. Situated on a hill, hundreds of people huddled together, seeking shelter under a sparse scattering of trees. Some of the Mien came into the camps with all their silver, but many were quite poor and had to leave what little they had to the communists. Yoon Choy wove together many thin, long leaves to make large panels which he leaned together to make a triangular tent for privacy. Nothing could keep out the stench. Human feces were everywhere. When it rained, the mud and feces mixed and flooded in thick puddles often coursing through their little tent, now their only home.

When Mae went into labor with their first child, she, like her mother before her, stayed alone. But Mae had no comforts of her old home: the hard-packed dirt floor and the familiar surroundings that would help to ease the fears of the first-time mother. Only the stench of heated filth awaited her newborn. She braced herself for each wave of constricting pain. Yoon Choy waited outside, occasionally fearing the worst when he heard Mae's involuntary gasps, yet he hoped in this new life; a treasure of innocence and newness. He hoped for survival, and tried to push the fears away. Yoon Choy's older sister had died giving birth. She had called for help when she saw the baby's foot emerge first from between her legs, and died as her mother and sisters tried to pull the baby from her body. Sometimes when there was a breach birth, the women pulled wildly at the baby, even if limbs were torn off in the process. Although these thoughts swirled in his mind, Mae had no complications and a beautiful baby girl was born and placed in her arms.

Mae feared for her daughter's future. She had heard talk of being transferred to a better camp, and hoped that it would be soon.

CW and Lois at Chiangkham refugee camp (1979)

After a year, the Thai authorities and the United Nations moved some of the refugees to Ban Dorng Camp in the district of Chiang Khong. Others were moved to a camp called Ban Kae near the town of Chiangkham. This is where the Callaways did most of their refugee work, and this is where Yoon Choy and Mae were relocated.

The United Nations funded the building of longhouses with metal roofs for the Ban Kae Camp. Each extended family was given one small room. The Mien families were quite large, so this meant ten to fifteen people occupied just one room. Each longhouse held about 200 people. In their haste to build shelters for the camp, bulldozers flattened and cleared out all the trees, leaving only the hard red clay. During the rainy season the clay turned the entire camp into one horrible sticky, sinking mass. In the summer the shadeless wasteland was filled with the stifling stench of warmed excrement. The sun-heated monotony became a tangible blanket of depression and hopelessness.

*Mien carrying firewood near Chiangkham
refugee camp (1979)*

There was never enough food in the camps - very little rice
and almost no meat or vegetables. A very lucky family might have
two pounds of meat in a week. Often the Thai farmers would
come into the camp and sell their produce, but then only those
who had any money were able to buy. In desperation and sometimes out of sheer boredom, the men would sneak under the wire
fence in search of any work to help to feed their families. Often
Yoon Choy cut a section of fence and escaped to work in the fields
of rice, opium and corn, usually digging the ground with a big
pick for less than fifty cents a day. One day, Yoon Choy decided to
try to wait by the roadside for a car to pass and hitch a ride. He
was caught by the Thai border police and placed in a "jail cell" at
the center of the Chiang Khong camp. The "cell" consisted of four
walls about ten feet high made of wooden planks spaced about
four inches apart. There was no roof so the sun beat down its
punishing rays on Yoon Choy. Mae brought him water to drink
and some rice and pushed it through the wide openings between
the planks. Yoon Choy was angry at the injustice, but the 100°
weather sapped his strength and his indignity curled inward. Yoon
Choy wondered bitterly why a refugee ceases to be a person. He
lay on his side against one wall where there was a sliver of shade
and tried to sleep away his pain. After twenty-four hours, he was

released to work to build a house. He worked for no pay since he was technically a prisoner.

*"The boy soldier," Yoon
Choy (here called Yuen
Leung Foo) registered
to immigrate to
USA in 1978*

Many of the villagers were severely malnourished when they arrived in the camp. Lois estimated that nearly half of the refugees had pink eye and about a third had symptoms of malaria. There were deaths daily, and it was exhausting and often discouraging work. Nurse Dorothy Uhlig maintained the Christian Clinic in Chiangkham during the week but on weekends, she went out to Ban Kae camp with the Callaways. They would take whatever helpers would come along.

C.W. stood in their midst. His tall figure was an easy beacon to find. "We are here with medicine," he called out. People gathered around him. Two lines were set up, one for pink eye, and one for malaria. C.W. asked a few simple questions to determine their symptoms, gave them a number, and had them stand in one of the two lines. Sometimes he could tell just by looking at them and pointed to the right line.

Yoon Choy spent much of his day watching his little daughter,

Yien, a joy and a brightness to him. Mae was expecting their second child soon and needed rest. Despite the horrific conditions of the camp, Yien grew, smiled, loved, and somehow even thrived. When she turned two, Yien suddenly fell gravely ill. The usually energetic and expressive child could hardly move. She refused food and water. Yoon Choy and Mae sought out the shamans and asked them to perform the rituals for her healing. Their meager savings were spent on buying live chickens for sacrifice. She didn't talk and didn't cry, only an occasional quiet moan; breathing took all her effort.

*Lois and CW with Mien Christian refugees
at Chiangkham camp (1979)*

When the shaman killed a chicken they carefully peeled back the flesh of the thigh to discern whether or not the child was curable, or if it is an evil spirit hurting the child. A small stick was used to peel the flesh and to find needle-sized holes in the thighbone. The holes in the thighbone gave spiritual indications of healing. If a hole was found in the middle, all was well. One end of the bone represented the head; the other end represented the leg. If no hole was found on the head side of the bone, it is determined that the child cannot be healed. Shaman after shaman sacrificed chicken after chicken and there was no hole to be found on the head side of the bone.

"Your child cannot be healed."

"She will die."

Those words hung like a lead chain on Yoon Choy's heart and tore open an inward rage. The old ways did nothing but waste money on many chickens. He was sick of the filth of the camp and the old ways that brought nothing. Nothing green ever grew in the red clay soil, there was no work to do, there was no purpose, a man was punished for wanting to work to provide for his family, nothing good could come of this place. He wanted all the horrible things to stop and he wanted his daughter to live, and grow and flourish. He wanted something new; something life-giving, something that breathed of goodness and hope, and he wanted it all for Yien. Sometimes he went to listen to the "Jesus Man" talk about God, and Yoon Choy wanted to speak to him. He and the "Jesus Lady" seemed so helpful and kind, but it was night and they had gone home. Yoon Choy knew of two Mien men who had given up ancestor and demon worship because they believed in this God Jesus. They were no longer afraid of the spirits. He stumbled between the longhouses to find them in the darkness. They came immediately and prayed for little Yien. Yoon Choy and Mae listened as the men told them that the Lord God could help them. As they prayed the power of God touched them both and they cried out to be saved and to save their daughter. The next morning Yien woke up and asked for some milk. Yien was healed.

When they next saw Mother Teacher, although she still looked large and sometimes frightening, they knew her God could be trusted. Perhaps so could she.

Chapter 15

Princess Mother

L ois looked into the eyes of the villagers. Once peacefully independent, they had survived for centuries in the security of tradition and clarity of routine. Now their eyes seemed clouded and lost. Each day in the camp was the same. If on rare occasions there were no sicknesses to be cared for there was still hardly a reason to be alive. They had no land and were desperate for income. The purposeless and hopelessness that the villagers faced each morning weighed heavily on Lois' heart, and she knew something had to be done.

Somewhere she remembered a brief exchange with M'Lou, back in old Tzanfuville in the Cabin in the Clouds. With an inspired clarity, Lois could once again envision M'Lou lifting her leg up and saying, "...but can you do this?" as she pointed to her embroidered trousers. Lois recalled her voice, full of pride, and her triumphant smile that cut an orange-wedge crescent across her tiny face. Recalling this picture made Lois smile too.

Lois started the "Mien Handicraft Project" with just one family. It grew to several more. She appointed two supervisors in two different refugee camps. World Vision helped to fund the sewing schools. They made tablecloths, purses, neckties, bordered jackets and skirts in an assortment of colorful patterns. The project became a means for the Mien to become financially independent and gradually pull away from the lucrative opium fields. Some anthropologists, however, were angered because she was tampering with the culture.

Mien women embroidering in refugee camp (1979)

"Keep the embroidery for what it was intended, it was meant to be worn on their own cultural outfits," they would say.

"How much money will that bring in?" asked Lois. And she kept on going to help both those who were Thai citizens as well as those who were refugees from Laos.

Since the refugees were not allowed to leave the camp, C.W. and Lois carted the products to the International School at Bangkok to sell at their handicraft fair. The Thai generally looked down on the mountain villagers as a whole, and wanted nothing to do with their handicrafts. For the most part, the best clients were buyers overseas, back in the States. Her best contact, however, was made through her son, Mark.

Mark, second of the five children spoke Thai fluently. His linguistic skills made him a valuable asset to various organizations. He worked for the U.S. Aid program in cooperation with the Thai government, and later for the United States Military Intelligence. As the C.I.A. tried to determine how to work against the communist insurgence, Mark worked as a translator and liaison between the United States government and the local village people. His least favorite task was to escort visitors by helicopter to familiarize them with the region. On one such excursion, a drug expert from Washington D.C. looked around at the beautiful poppy fields in which they had landed.

"These people sure must like flowers."

Mark replied, "They're opium poppies, sir."

The drug expert replied, "Opium poppies, how do you like that."

Mark had regular contact with the Thai border police as well.

The King of Thailand's mother was the patron of the border police. She had flown on several helicopter visits to various villages, bringing gifts to the children and had shown an interest in the "Mien Handicraft Project."

The King's mother was referred to as the "Princess Mother" since she was not actually of royal blood herself. Her son had become the heir to the throne through several defaults. His father died, to be succeeded by his uncle, but his uncle fled the country. This left his older cousin, but he also died, leaving him the eldest male of royal blood. Although he was not groomed to be king, he found himself ruling all of Thailand.

One day, the Princess Mother sent her personal secretary to check on the embroidery project when the Callaways were living in Chiangkham. Lois ran outside amidst the crazy beating racket of helicopter blades. The secretary, a man who was known for his efficiency and directness had landed his helicopter in her backyard. This man also carried a royal title, MR (an honorable abbreviation for prince) Diskul Disanadda.

The Princess Mother sent two people to assist MR Diskul Disanadda on his visit to Mother Teacher. His secretary, a Thai lady was introduced, followed by a high ranking officer of the border police. They met in the home and discussed and exchanged ideas. After some time, MR Diskul Disanadda announced that he felt tired and asked for a pillow. Lois invited him to use the bed, but he politely declined and stretched himself out on the floor beside the little meeting. Later, when the police officer had returned from business in town and saw the prince asleep on the floor, he said, "He looks very comfortable."

"You are welcome to use the bed."

"Thank you, a pillow will be enough."

The officer situated himself on the floor near the prince and promptly fell asleep himself. Meanwhile, Lois and the secretary kept ideas stirring.

Inspiration hit Lois, "Why not have an evening time where some Mien women can go sell their crafts in the city?"

"It is a fine idea, but will they come?"

Lois knew that the Thai were not especially welcoming to the mountain villagers. If someone of stature were to stand by these handicrafts...

"I wonder how open the Princess Mother would be to such an idea."Lois found out how open the Princess Mother was one day when they met MR Diskul Disanadda one day over lunch.

"The Princess Mother is staying in a nearby government house after visiting a refugee camp. She invites you for dinner."

Lois protested," I don't have any appropriate clothes."

"Just wear your pajamas then," he joked.

At the dinner, C.W. and Lois were seated with MR Diskul Disanadda and several members of the Thai Border Police who were heavily decorated with gold braid and plastered with medals. Guests were taking their turn visiting with the Princess Mother at her table. Finally, MR Diskul Disanadda leaned forward.

"The Princess Mother will see you now."

After a bit of small talk, Lois ventured to say, "It is a beautiful dress you have on, Your Royal Highness, but you really ought to have some Mien embroidery on it." She could tell that C.W. was a bit nervous at her boldness, but all laughed when the Princess Mother replied, "If someone would give me some, I'd certainly wear it." And she did.

Once the royal family of Thailand got involved, Mien embroidery became phenomenally popular. The Prince's wife opened up a shop to sell handicrafts in Bangkok. There was even a fashion show sponsored by the Royal Family featuring Thai movie stars as models. Each model was adorned in Mien handcrafted embroidery. Even some thirty years later, many Thai women at formal gatherings still wear black jackets with hand-embroidered Mien edging.

Since the Princess Mother had a special interest in the border police, they desired to promote their police activities. They too, opened a handicraft shop in Chiang Mai which the King attended for the dedication. C.W. and Lois were asked to be in the receiving line.

There were already accomplished teak woodcarvers and artisans working in silver and other craftsmen in Chiang Mai. The development of the Mien handicrafts and then those of other mountain tribes led eventually to the establishment of the Chiang Mai Night Bazaar, which continues to this day. That bazaar is held every night and it continues until well after dark. Thousands of western tourists visit there each night to purchase the Mien embroidery and other fine works of local art.

After the Callaways had moved back to the States, they continued regular contact with the Mien refugees that received sponsorship to the United States. At any given Mien gathering, at least one woman would take Lois by the hands and tell her how the embroidery project kept her hopes up in the monotony and drudgery of the refugee camps. Lois marveled as she held those precious hands. It seemed like yesterday that she was hiking up the mountain trails and trying to win the Mien people's trust; trying to make her eyes seem a bit less yellow. Now the Mien were her friends; her family, and rather than adjusting to the smoky indoor fire and dirt floors, she considered now how she might help her Mien friends to adjust to concrete, lights, and red tape.

Christian Church Missionaries, Chiang Mai Thailand 1961
*Back row L-R: Mark Sterling, David Filbeck, Mel Byers,
Don Byers, Lillie & Harry Schaefer, Dorothy & Garland
Bare, Lois & C.W. Callaway
Seated: Deloris Filbeck, June Byers, Roberta Byers,
Emma Schaefer, Dorothy Uhlig, Dorothy Sterling,
Imogene Williams
On ground and in arms and center:
Children of missionaries*

The Callaway family (1961)

The Callaway family at David and Cathy's wedding
(1982)

Missionary Co-workers (2004)
L-R: Mel & June Byers, Don & Roberta Byers,
Imogene Williams, Dorothy Uhlig

Chapter 16

The Wedding

CW Prays at Jenifer &
Chai's wedding 1998

1998. It has been nearly twenty years that Yoon Choy, Mae, and their children have been in the United States. Mother Teacher is gone. She died in a car accident. C.W. stands before them now preparing to speak to a large crowd gathered for their only daughter's wedding. Yien. The one that God saved from death in the Thai refugee camp.

C.W. still holds himself tall, only now with a slight tremble to his movements. He speaks gently in Mien.

"Remember how God saved Yien. He is faithful. He is good. Trust in Him. He has brought Yien to this happy day."

There is singing and food, the peppered meats, and cooked greens, and when the festivities are over, guests mingle and hover over Father Teacher. Reminiscing begins.

Yoon Choy with his daughter Jenifer
1998

They remember Mother Teacher. On September 5, 1996, Lois was driving on the long, road home from the doctor's. It was hot in Vallejo; nothing unusual. C.W. had offered to drive, but she said she'd rather have the cupboard shelf repaired that he was working on, and as she had made the trip many times alone in the past, no one worried. The doctor said her heart was doing okay. What the test results couldn't detect was that Lois' heart was broken up for the lost. Her heart was so full of love for her Mien family and loved ones; maybe it only took a nudge for it to break open. On the way home, she inexplicably hit an oncoming car, and then another. The others involved in the accident lived, but she did not. Her heart stopped beating. The same body that trudged up the mountains of Thailand, and maneuvered through the freeway mazes of California, had suddenly ceased. Now she is home, at the very time that He ordained it. She is finally home. The heavenly Father has given her rest, and she can smile at her life.

Lois' final home on earth was in California. Here among the refugees of war, she saw the Lord's hand move generously in the hearts of the Mien. The faith that she desired to cultivate in this relatively unknown tribal group had begun to take root.

Andrew Lai remembers Lois:

Lois (on right) with Forwarding Agent Benette Rhoades, Amarillo, Texas (1975)

"In my family we called her "Grandma" because she was so dear to us and to our children. She was our mentor, our teacher, our encourager and many times more than a friend. Mrs. Callaway loved butterflies. To me she represented the grace and the beauty of a butterfly but she moved like a hummingbird. One minute she was with the school board urging them to have more tutors for bilingual students, the next minute she would be in the ladies' home Bible study, teaching the Mien ladies how to deal with family issues in the light of the Scripture. Then she would still come to my house for a prayer meeting. She prayed for the Mien church a lot. She was the one who taught us always start the day with prayer. On the cover of her Bible she had a poem about never to start a day without praying. She was a super prayer warrior.

"She said the Mien people have a difficult time in telling you their addresses... "I live beside the big tree." I said, "What if Caltrans cut the tree down?" Mrs. Callaway said, "Then I guess you cannot find the house without the address." In her Bible she underlined Psalm 76:2 and wrote by the margin "the address of God." You can be 100% sure that she is now at the right address in heaven.

"Mrs. Callaway loved praise singing. In the morning worship she usually sat somewhere there. She always raised her hands worshiping the Lord. What a glorious sight to see her now raising her hands among the angels worshiping the Lord in the presence of Jesus. I knew her so well. I know she wants us to celebrate with her now and not to mourn like those without hope. She also would want us to be strong in faith and not be discouraged. I can hear her whispering to all of us urging us to continue the work that she started. The best way to remember Mrs. Callaway is to serve the Lord in the way that she did. She loved us so much because she first loved the Lord. To me she is the supreme example of faithfulness, commitment and most of all Agape Love. She will always be in our memories for eternity. She would always be our grandma, mother, teacher and good friend."

C.W. finally spoke…

"Even at those midnight hours when my wandering thoughts would not allow me to sleep His word has brought comfort. And His Spirit has given the confidence that I will see Lois again.

"Having heard the inconsolable wailing of many in the Orient who are without this hope, I am all the more grateful for the privilege of knowing Jesus and through His resurrection knowing that we too will live again," and he shared this poem by Lois written on the occasion of their own wedding:

CW with Lois wearing
Mien vest (1985)

We joined our hands that happy night;
His hand was laid o'er all.
We sealed the vows with wedding kiss;
His Spirit hovered o'er.
Two hearts that beat as one, O Lord,
Two heads that bow as one,
Two lives that blend together
In Thy all-perfect love.
As hand in hand we walk, O Lord,
Together seek Thy will;
What more could mortals ask, Dear God,
These hearts could hold no more.

...Then someday will come the glad moment
With rapture I'll see His dear face.
That day I'll be changed in a twinkling,
Transported to His own dear Place.
My heaven-freed soul will behold Him,
His glorious thunder of Power.
As never before my heart will be knowing
'Twas all but a whisper of God.

Lois Callaway, 1921 – 1996

End Notes:

Chapter 1
[1] Chao, Youd Sinh; Southeast Asian Cultures (With a Focus on the
Iu-Mien)
Legends passed on through the Mien oral tradition have some
variations, dates are often conjectural.

Chapter 4
[2] Robbins, Christopher, <u>The Ravens</u>, p. 132.
[3] Robbins, Christopher, <u>The Ravens</u>, p. 52

Chapter 12
[4] Karnow, Stanley; <u>Vietnam: A History</u>, The Viking Press, ©1983,
pp. 10-11.

Chapter 14
[5] J.M. Roberts in his book <u>History of the World</u>,

Mother Teacher Community Development Inc. (MTCD)

Jeni Callaway Goddard was born in Thailand. She and husband John Goddard now minister there in the area where she was born. In honor of her mother, Lois Callaway, they with others have established this development ministry. MTCD works in an advisory role and through sponsorship of a variety of community based programs to address local needs. MTCD's role is to promote sustainable growth in areas of family life, community based economic development and spiritual life. Some major projects are …

Chiangkham Youth Development Center (CYDC)
& CYDC Crafts Project,
Hydroponics Gardening Project,
Welding and Brick making Project,
Ban Timothy (Timothy House), Co-op development fund,
Mother Teacher Crafts, Literacy Development Project,
Mother Teacher Training Centers

Why this ministry

Many immigrant communities in the USA are plagued by gangs and other obstacles to family and community life. In S.E. Asia drugs and the Aids pandemic have destroyed the family structure in most rural villages, leaving many families without fathers or mothers to care for their children. Children are at risk of being sold into prostitution and young girls are often forced to marry an older man for money. The social service network does not have the ability to deal with these problems.

Christ said "..when you do it unto the least of these you have done it unto me."

How to Contact us

Mother Teacher Community Development Inc.
2355 Camp Baker Rd.
Medford Or. 97501 USA
Phone : 541-512-9781

Web site : www.MotherTeacher.org

John and Jeni Goddard
PO Box 5 , Chiangkham
56110 Phayao, THAILAND

Printed in the United States
24112LVS00005B/181-636

9 781594 678882